Writing the Senior Executi~
Traditional ECQs and Five-Page SES Resume

The New
SES
Application

2nd Edition

KATHRYN TROUTMAN
DIANE HUDSON

Federal Career Training Institute

A Division of The Resume Place, Inc.
1012 Edmondson Avenue, Catonsville, MD 21228
Phone: (888) 480-8265
www.fedjobtraining.com
Email: ses@fedjobtraining.com

Printed in the United States of America
Copyright © 2011, 2016 by Kathryn Troutman

ISBN-10: 0984667156
ISBN-13: 978-0-9846671-5-4

We have been careful to provide accurate federal job search information in this book, but it is possible that errors and omissions may have been introduced, as requirements change freequently.

Sample resumes are real but fictionalized. All federal applicants have given their permission for their resumes to be used as samples for this publication. Privacy policy is strictly enforced.

Publication Team

Publisher: Kathryn Troutman

Developmental Editors: Emily Troutman and Paulina Chen

Cover and Page Design / Layout: Paulina Chen

Curriculum Development, Exercises, and Design Contributions: Emily Troutman and Nicole Schultheis

OPM SES Consultant and Contributor: Paul Thompson

Proofreader: Pamela Sikora

Indexer: Pilar Wyman

Table of Contents

Introduction

The Senior Executive Service Application—being about 21 pages, on average—is the BIGGEST hurdle that a senior executive will have to jump over to enter into the SES. As SES ECQ Writing Instructors throughout many government agencies, we often see these common mistakes:

- Focusing on management, instead of leadership
- Using the terms "we", the "team", the "staff", rather than saying "I" achieved the results
- Singling out their most important accomplishments
- Talking in generalities instead of about the specifics of their mission, budget, staff, resources, and contracts

The challenges facing executives since the first edition of this book have become MORE challenging. This year, the U.S. government will have to face issues such as: achieving the 10% budget cuts of sequestration; cutting contracts and restricting the performance of the civil service staff left behind; downturn of the war and the lessening operations and business services for the war; hiring and caring for veterans and implementing new veterans programs.

The SES applications and ECQs need to reflect the challenges in America. The ECQs need to be written about individual leadership, keeping America safe, staying within budget, and providing Americans the services they need, as well as the daily operations of a large government agency.

-- Be inspired to lead, Kathryn Troutman

During the past ten years, I have trained scores of GS-15s, GS-14s, and even GS-12s and GS-13s and equivalents to write their Senior Executive Service resumes and Executive Core Qualification statements, from across the government and industry, using this book as the course curriculum. The SES application package is the pinnacle of career search documents—a "super resume"—fully articulating a career history of top-level leadership accomplishments.

I have led numerous ECQ writing classes and webinars, and the stories and examples that participants regale are inspiring! Listening to participants' stories is like delving into a novel: one client traveled to the space station seven times; one built a reservoir to capture rain water run-off; one designed an emergency management program that became a model for other agencies; one created a transportation system for troops in Iraq and Afghanistan; and one launched a non-profit for children of wounded warriors. I could go on and on describing the stories that participants share in the classes.

The New SES Application is written in a user-friendly format, and is chock full of examples to guide you in writing your SES application and prepare for the structured interview. The format and case studies described in the book are the tools you need to learn how to write your SES resume package. Refer often to the Leadership Journey chart to diagram your career succession plan to attain SES.

-- Best wishes for continued career success, Diane Hudson

Warm-Up Exercise: Accomplishment Freewriting

Use the space below to practice writing one of your significant leadership accomplishments in the CCAR format. You can also use an online CCAR builder on the Resume Place website; type in your accomplishment story and have it emailed to you for cutting and pasting.

ECQ Title:

Challenge

Context

Link to free CCAR Builder: www.resume-place.com/ccar-builder/

Note: The OPM SES CCAR puts "Challenge" first, and the non-SES CCAR puts "Context" first.

Action

Result

Chapter One

About the SES

The Senior Executive Service (SES) positions in government are the highest level positions next to Presidential Appointee careers. The application for the SES positions is long, precise, complex, and highly competitive. The bottom line is that if you would like to be leader in government, then the SES application is your next career writing task.

Considering these challenging leadership responsibilities, are you ready to lead? If so, this book can help you write the SES application and prove your ability to perform these leadership responsibilities:

Director, Institutional Services, Department of Education, Office of Postsecondary Education. The Director plays a critical leadership role in advancing postsecondary education by working on a national scale to improve the capacity and performance of colleges and universities.

Deputy Administrator of Coal Mine Safety and Health, Department of Labor, Mine Safety and Health Administration. Because of intense Congressional interest regarding CMS&H, incumbent must apply intimate knowledge of Department of Labor policies and objectives and in-depth understanding and insight to objectives of the Mine Safety and Health Administration to ensure that all Congressional correspondence and inquiries are responded to fully and expeditiously.

SUPERINTENDENT, MARINE METEOROLOGY DIVISION. Dept of the Navy, Naval Research Laboratory. The Superintendent is responsible for the overall planning and direction of a coordinated research and development program in meteorology and atmospheric sciences designed to meet the present and future needs of the Navy.

Deputy Division Director, Division of Advanced Cyberinfrastructure, National Science Foundation. Serves as a member of the CISE leadership team and as a Foundation spokesperson in the area of cyberinfrastructure for research. The Division of Advanced Cyberinfrastructure coordinates and supports the exploration, acquisition, development and provision of state-of-the-art cyberinfrastructure resources, tools and services essential to the conduct of 21st century science and engineering research and education.

How to Find SES Vacancies

All SES vacancies are advertised on the Office of Personnel Management's (OPM) USAJOBS website: www.usajobs.gov. From this site, you can browse for SES vacancy announcements and submit your applications.

What Are the Differences Between SES, ST, and SL Positions?

Senior Executive Service (SES) positions are above GS-15 or equivalent and involve one or more of the criteria set forth in the United States Code (5 USC 3132), such as directing the work of an organization and monitoring progress toward organizational goals.

Scientific and professional (ST) positions are competitive service positions above the GS-15 level involving high-level research and development. These positions do not require OPM approval.

Senior level (SL) positions are also above the GS-15 level but usually do not meet the SES criteria and do not involve the research and development responsibilities of ST positions. SL positions may be in either the competitive or excepted service.

SES Salary Information

The following table shows the range of salaries for SES members for 2015. SES members are not eligible for locality pay adjustments.

View this table at: www.opm.gov/policy-data-oversight/pay-leave/salaries-wages/salary-tables/15Tables/exec/html/ES.aspx

Other pay tables for executive and senior level federal employees can be found at: www.opm.gov/policy-data-oversight/pay-leave/salaries-wages/2015/executive-senior-level

Pay & Leave
SALARIES & WAGES

Salary Table No. 2015-ES

Rates of Basic Pay for Members of the Senior Executive Service (SES)
Effective January 2015

Structure of the SES Pay System	Minimum	Maximum
Agencies with a Certified SES Performance Appraisal System	$121,956	$183,300
Agencies without a Certified SES Performance Appraisal System	$121,956	$168,700

"Most SES candidates and executives do not apply for the SES positions based on salary. They apply for SES positions in order to lead and direct change toward new and improved programs and services for Americans; communicate with Congress regarding important programs within an agency; attempt to solve big problems in government regulations and financial operations; and overall use their subject-matter expertise to make a real difference for Americans and the U.S. Government with savings of cost, improved performance of employees, resource management and technical direction. APPLY NOW! America needs top decisive leaders!"

-- Kathryn Troutman, SES Executive Leadership Coach

SES Federal Candidate Development Program (CDP)

The federal government offers an SES Candidate Development Program, based on the five Executive Core Qualifications (ECQs), to foster future federal agency leadership and prepare candidates for immediate entry into SES. This 12- to 18-month program is available by competition (from various agencies) for GS-15/equivalents. The model includes feedback-intensive mentoring and networking components to further assist candidates in their developmental journey to seek SES.

There is good news for candidates who successfully complete the program and obtain certification of ECQs by an SES Qualifications Review Board (QRB)—they may be selected for an SES position anywhere in the federal government without further competition/review of ECQs. As part of their leadership journey, GS-13s and 14s may want to include the CDP in their professional development plan target for when they attain the GS-15 level.

See more sample SES CDP announcements on pages 72 and 142-145.

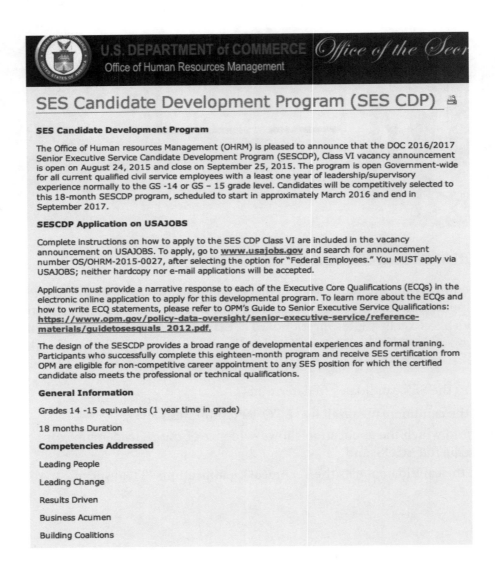

Federal Career Training Institute | www.fedjobtraining.com

The OPM Qualifications Review Board SES Recruitment and Review Process

Agency Executive Resources Board

After initial screening by the human resources office to eliminate obviously unqualified applicants, SES applications are given a first hard look by a group of reviewers consisting of either the agency's SES Executive Resources Board (ERB) or, more typically, a panel of SES members acting on its behalf. The ERB rates and ranks the applicants and identifies the best-qualified candidates to move forward.

The ERB evaluates the SES candidates to determine:

1. whether the candidate meets all five ECQs at a minimum level;
2. the extent to which the application shows evidence of the 28 leadership competencies that underlie the ECQS; and
3. how well the candidate meets the Technical Qualifications (TQs) specific to the position.

Additional Assessments, Including the SES Behavior-Based Interview

The agency may require additional assessments as part of the screening process. For example, structured interviews are becoming increasingly more common and are required by OPM when the application is resume-based. Additional screening may also include a writing sample, assessment test, reference check, or secondary interview. The executive to whom the selectee will report may also interview best-qualified candidates as determined by the panel and may make a recommendation to the full ERB. The ERB will deliberate on all of the information and send forward one or more candidates to the selecting official (usually the agency head) for a tentative selection, subject to certification by an OPM-led Qualifications Review Board.

Office of Personnel Management's Qualifications Review Board (QRB)

The critical last step in the SES selection process is certification by the QRB. This group— administered by the Office of Personnel Management—is a rotating panel of three volunteer Senior Executive Service members who assemble once or twice a week to review tentative selections to the SES. The QRB provides an independent peer review of SES candidates for their first appointment to the SES. An SES candidate cannot be appointed to the SES until the QRB certifies his or her Executive Core Qualifications. The QRB helps ensure that the agency's selection process was unbiased and that technical skills do not outweigh leadership expertise in the selection of new senior executives.

Ordinarily the QRB primarily focuses on reviewing the ECQs, but in the case of a resume-based selection it must rely on the candidate's resume and other information provided by the agency, such as notes from the candidate's structured interview.

If your application is forwarded to the QRB and evaluated, here are the possible outcomes:

- If the QRB sees in your certification package that you have the leadership capabilities for an SES position in government, you will receive a notice that you are certified. This QRB certification will then result in your being hired into the position. The certification is good for life (assuming you complete successfully the one year probation period), even if you leave the federal government. Also, once you occupy a career SES position, you may seek other SES positions without resubmitting ECQs.

- If your certification package is disapproved by the Board, the selecting agency will receive detailed information about what is missing or otherwise insufficient (see Chapter 8). If the disapproval is based on review of your written ECQ narratives, you will be given approximately four to eight weeks to resubmit the ECQs. Similarly, when a resume-based selection is initially disapproved, the agency may submit additional evidence in order to make the case for certification.

- Resubmissions are successful in most cases, but if your submission is disapproved again, the agency has several options, such as re-advertising the position, changing the classification, or submitting a request for a "developmental" SES appointment, which if successful means final certification would be contingent on your participating in training or other developmental activities.

Executive Core Qualifications (ECQs)

The most challenging part of the SES application is developing and writing the ECQs. They are narrative statements, written in the first person, that include clear examples demonstrating the competencies and characteristics needed to build executive leadership in a federal corporate culture that drives for results, serves customers, and builds successful teams and coalitions within and outside the organization.

Possession of the Executive Core Qualifications is required for entry to the Senior Executive Service. The ECQs also guide the development of those already in Senior Executive Service positions.

As part of their succession planning, some agencies are also beginning to look for the leadership skills required for executives earlier in the selection process, including using the ECQs in the selection of GS-14 and GS-15 level positions. This is particularly true of selection for agency SES Candidate Development Programs.

Executive Core Qualifications are the primary selection criteria for the SES. While technical job-specific qualifications are important, the essence of the SES is the ability to lead, as articulated in the leadership skills that comprise the Executive Core Qualifications.

Leading Change	This core qualification involves the ability to bring about strategic change, both within and outside the organization, to meet organizational goals. Inherent to this ECQ is the ability to establish an organizational vision and to implement it in a continuously changing environment.
Leading People	This core qualification involves the ability to lead people toward meeting the organization's vision, mission, and goals. Inherent to this ECQ is the ability to provide an inclusive workplace that fosters the development of others, facilitates cooperation and teamwork, and supports constructive resolution of conflicts.
Results Driven	This core qualification involves the ability to meet organizational goals and customer expectations. Inherent to this ECQ is the ability to make decisions that produce high-quality results by applying technical knowledge, analyzing problems, and calculating risks.
Business Acumen	This core qualification involves the ability to manage human, financial, and information resources strategically.
Building Coalitions	This core qualification involves the ability to build coalitions internally and with other federal agencies, state and local governments, nonprofit and private sector organizations, foreign governments, or international organizations to achieve common goals.

Leadership and Fundamental Competencies

Competencies are the personal and professional attributes that are critical to successful performance in the SES. There are 28 competencies. Twenty-two of them are the specific competencies for the Executive Core Qualifications (ECQs), with each ECQ representing a "bundle" of related competencies from the 22. The remaining six are the fundamental competencies and together serve as the foundation for all of the ECQs.

A well-prepared ECQ statement reflects the underlying ECQ-specific competencies (e.g., "Leading Change" reflects creativity and innovation, external awareness, etc.). Because the fundamental competencies are cross-cutting, they should be addressed throughout the complete ECQ narrative. It is not necessary to address them directly as long as the narrative, in its totality, shows mastery of these fundamental competencies. Experience and training that strengthen and demonstrate the competencies will enhance a candidate's overall qualifications for the SES.

The Six Cross-Cutting Fundamental Competencies

Interpersonal Skills	Treats others with courtesy, sensitivity, and respect. Considers and responds appropriately to the needs and feelings of different people in different situations. **{Writers' Tip:** This competency can be easily addressed in Leading People and Building Coalitions stories by describing how you interact with other people.}
Oral Communication	Makes clear and convincing oral presentations. Listens effectively; clarifies information as needed. **{Writers' Tip:** This competency can be addressed in many ECQs—examples of conducting negotiations or briefing leadership validate oral communications.}
Integrity/Honesty	Behaves in an honest, fair, and ethical manner. Shows consistency in words and actions. Models high standards of ethics. **{Writers' Tip:** An example of integrity and honesty may be found in a story about conflict resolution or funds administration/financial stewardship.}
Written Communication	Writes in a clear, concise, organized, and convincing manner for the intended audience. **{Writers' Tip:** This competency can be described in a story about preparing high-level presentations and reports for use by Congress; legal briefs, meeting agendas, budget justifications, contracts, and/or books and peer-reviewed publications.}
Continual Learning	Assesses and recognizes own strengths and weaknesses; pursues self-development. **{Writers' Tip:** Continual Learning may be addressed in examples of higher education, attendance and participation at high-level symposia, or completion of an SES development program.}
Public Service Motivation	Shows a commitment to serve the public. Ensures that actions meet public needs; aligns organizational objectives and practices with public interests. **{Writers' Tip:** Public Service Motivation is expressed in continually serving customers—being on the forefront of developing and implementing programs to serve the public. It may also be expressed in supporting management and subordinates to create successful programs.}

Developing Leadership Competencies

This Leadership Journey chart on the next page was developed by the Office of Personnel Management. The chart is used to help individuals and agencies build the development segment of their Succession Plan. The graphic lays out the 28 OPM leadership competencies. The competencies serve as the roadmap for leadership development.

The core leadership competencies are basic competencies for all employees. Research indicates that without these core competencies, success at upper levels is not possible.

The graphic illustrates the customary levels of management and leadership. Associated with each level are related competencies that are critical for success at that level and form a developmental step for the next level of management or leadership. There are key experiences at each level that are designed to reinforce the associated competencies.

The major test of SES readiness is in the accomplishments that you will write for your ECQs. Are they at the Leading Organizations level? Are they at the Managing Programs level? The ECQs will determine if you are qualified today for an SES position, or qualified for an SES Candidate Development Program, in which you will participate in developmental assignments and executive leadership training for up to two years before you can submit your ECQs to OPM for certification as an SES member. Candidates who successfully complete the program and obtain certification by an SES Qualifications Review Board (QRB) may be selected for an SES position anywhere in the federal government without further review of ECQs.

The SES vacancy announcements requiring the five-page SES federal resume state: "It is highly recommended that your resume address your accomplishments in these specific competency areas." For the traditional 10-page ECQs, the HR specialists recommend: "The ECQs assess the broad executive skills needed to succeed in the Senior Executive Service (SES). The narrative should demonstrate the necessary level of management skills, characteristics, qualities, specialized knowledge, and technical competence that would indicate successful performance in the SES. This evidence must include clear and concise examples that emphasize your level of responsibilities, scope and complexity of the programs managed, program accomplishments, policy initiatives, and level of contacts."

In order to qualify for SES Career Development Programs, you will need to write your ECQ accomplishments at the Managing Programs and Managing People levels. Applicants must demonstrate possession of or the potential to develop the five ECQs in their SES five-page resume, or in their traditional ECQ essays. The SES HR Recruiters say that "you must have knowledge of management/leadership practices and principles, and possess the potential to function at an executive level. You must also have the ability to implement equal employment opportunity."

In order to qualify for SES positions, your ECQ accomplishments should be at the Leading Organizations/Executive level, where you are leading change, leading people, achieving results, managing business operations, and building coalitions.

The Leadership Journey

Focusing Your Learning for Career and Organizational Success

Executive
External Awareness
Vision
Strategic Thinking
Entrepreneurship
Resilience
Decisiveness

Leading Organizations

Manager
Technology Management
Financial Management
Creativity & Innovation
Partnering
Political Savvy
Flexibility

Managing Programs

Supervisor
Human Capital Management
Leveraging Diversity
Conflict Management
Developing Others
Problem Solving

Managing People

Team Leader Project Manager
Team Building
Customer Service
Technical Credibility
Accountability
Influencing/ Negotiating

Managing Projects

Management Levels

Fundamental Competencies

Interpersonal Skills	Oral Communication	Continual Learning
Written Communication	Integrity/Honesty	Public Service Motivation

Managing Yourself

Chapter Two

Writing Your Top Ten List of Accomplishments

Step-by-Step Process of Building an ECQ Narrative

1. SHORT TOP TEN LIST
Make a list of ten of your BEST leadership accomplishments from the past ten years. Use short descriptions.

2. MAP YOUR TOP TEN LIST
Match up your Top Ten list to the five ECQs (two per ECQ).

3. CCAR FORMAT TOP TEN LIST
Build out each accomplishment into the OPM-required Challenge-Context-Action-Results (CCAR) format.

4. KEYWORDS
Add keywords from the vacancy announcement and the 28 Leadership Competencies.

5. COMPLETE YOUR NARRATIVE
Write out your Top Ten in an executive narrative writing style to tell a compelling story. Use Plain Language. Edit and proofread.

Getting Ready to Write

Getting started with a writing project is often the toughest part.

The first step in drafting your SES application is to develop a list of your most significant accomplishments. We call this your "Top Ten List of Accomplishments." Many of our clients and class participants have difficulty developing a solid list of achievements to demonstrate their leadership capabilities. Your goal in this step is to cultivate a variety of examples that highlights the breadth and the depth of your leadership skills and proves that you possess the ECQ leadership competencies.

Assignment:
Your Top Ten List of Accomplishments–Short Version

Thank you David Letterman for creating the Top Ten List for America every weekday evening for 33 years. This same Top Ten List approach can be utilized very effectively for starting to write your ECQs. Your Top Ten List should include your most memorable, challenging, effective, meaningful, and recognized accomplishments.

Draft your first list of your best accomplishments that you have achieved for the last five to ten years of your career. This short version of your Top Ten will eventually turn into the ten-page ECQs that are required by OPM for your SES application.

Brainstorm a list of your significant accomplishments (in a word processing file if possible). For each accomplishment, write a short paragraph to describe it. Do not worry about format at this stage; you are simply trying to generate ideas. Aim to have at least 10 solid examples, though it can be helpful to generate as many ideas as possible.

> **These accomplishments are NOT the tasks you perform in your job every day; in other words, it's not a job description. Think of specific examples to demonstrate that you have achieved leadership level accomplishments.**

Make sure to list specific projects and programs. You can also include longer-term initiatives or responsibilities. Examples from nonprofit or volunteer activities are acceptable, but they must be leadership examples, such as sitting on a Board of Directors for a large association.

Concentrate on the most recent 10 years. If you have a powerful and relevant example of leadership at the executive level prior to 10 years ago, you may use it as one of your examples, but be aware that the QRB is looking for the most recent examples of leadership to ensure, in part, that the candidate is aware of current events and changes in legislation and policies.

Try to include measurable results for each accomplishment. To get inspired, see the list of sample executive-worthy accomplishements on the next page (in no particular order).

Sample Top Ten List of Accomplishments–Short Version

This sample Top Ten List of Accomplishments are mapped on pages 28-29 and expanded using the CCAR format on pages 32-34.

1. Conceived the idea, developed a vision and strategic plan, and stood up the Iraqi Republic Railway, which became the first government agency in Iraq to generate revenue and become self-sustaining, providing relief to logistical planning and response to all categories of contingency situations in that region.

2. Provided planning and coordination guidance for military and DOD personnel and equipment for two joint federal and DOD emergency response exercises: SUDDEN RESPONSE (guided efforts of 143 emergency responders from NORTHCOM, FEMA and Region VII military personnel) and VIBRANT RESPONSE (a national training event involving 500+ DOD, federal, state and civilian emergency responders).

3. Represented the Air Force and senior government officials before the Governor and other agencies, committees, organizations, media, unions, and private organizations. Developed and promoted relationships with federal and state military, and civilian and interagency organizations including FEMA and the state Emergency Manager and staff. Guided official staff in obtaining DOD Title 10 support as needed for disasters. Advised the Governor on the status of the federal response.

4. Led the development of wilderness management plans for over 1.2 million acres of Congressionally designated wilderness through passage of two lands bills.

5. Led comprehensive change in managing BLM's Land and Water Conservation Fund (LWCF) within the Department of the Interior (DOI) and the initiative to gain full funding for the LWCF Program, which required completely transforming how all four affected land management agencies work together.

6. I reorganized the realty staff as part of an agency-wide transformation initiative designed to streamline staffing and identify opportunities to consolidate positions, especially in the Washington Office. In support of the Director, I recommended and implemented revisions to the organization that included eliminating certain positions, filling long vacant but vital positions, and utilizing alternative hiring authorities. My recommendations were incorporated into the transformed organization and approved by the agency's Executive Leadership Team.

7. I led a large organization with a budget of $100M, and 70 staff supporting 32,000 contracts throughout the Pacific region, reaching from Hawaii to Japan and satellite offices as far south as Australia, including the Pacific Headquarters. I introduced the concept of implementing Wide-Area Workflow (WAWF), a complete end-to-end processing of an invoice through to electronic payment, elevating the organization into the 21st century, by replacing antiquated technology and introducing automation that would create efficiencies enterprise-wide. After implementation interest penalty payments reduced 25% percent overall; invoice processing time initially reduced ~40% for contracts in the project.

8. The past couple years have been a time of enormous change in health care policy focused on the enactment of the Affordable Care Act (ACA). I facilitated health reform implementation efforts, and built and oversaw the policy coordination team necessary to meet the new health reform workload, as well as the ongoing workload of the agency to run Medicare, Medicaid and the Children's Health Insurance Program.

9. I assumed leadership as the Acting Director of the Office of Strategic Operations and Regulatory Affairs, inheriting an organization ranked 21 of 22 offices, according to the annual Human Capital survey. Via team building and professional development, I am resolving some of the lingering conflict and continue to better utilize the office's human resources. The office is becoming more cohesive and better at meeting customer needs, which directly affects how policy from my organization will impact the public. My efforts led to a high-functioning team, enabling us to meet the Administration's priorities. Almost three years into the implementation effort, with ongoing demands on the team and other offices actively recruiting my staff, there has been low turnover. The team is well respected, with all staff performance far exceeding expectations.

10. I directed a large, multidisciplinary, international, and geographically dispersed staff across eight countries. I oversaw a diverse 120-person organization including local nationals, third-country nationals, contractors, government civilians, and military members located in several countries spread across 18 military installations supporting three Combatant Commands. This was a difficult position. This diversity caused cultural differences that I managed on a daily basis to balance the working environment across the larger staffs.

Exercise: Your Short Top Ten List of Accomplishments

In the space below, record specific examples of your more recent leadership accomplishments. Remember, these accomplishments are NOT the tasks you perform in your job every day; in other words, it's not a job description.

Chapter Three

Mapping Your Top Ten List of Accomplishments

Study the ECQ Leadership Competencies to determine where your accomplishments fit into the five ECQs.

- If your accomplishment refers to CHANGE, creativity and innovation, resilience and strategic thinking, then this story will be LEADING CHANGE.

- If your accomplishment refers to PEOPLE, conflict with people, leveraging diversity, developing others, then this story will be LEADING PEOPLE.

- If your accomplishment is about RESULTS, accountability, customer service and entrepreneurship, then this story will be RESULTS DRIVEN.

- If your accomplishment is about BUSINESS, financial management, human capital management and technology, then the story will be BUSINESS ACUMEN.

- If your accomplishment is about PARTNERSHIPS, coalitions, political savvy and negotiating skills, then the story will be BUILDING COALITIONS.

Exercise: Mapping Accomplishments to the ECQs

After you have developed your Top Ten List of Accomplishments, it is time to begin to match your accomplishments to the ECQs. Below is an exercise to show you how this matching process works.

For each accomplishment below, please select an ECQ that is best demonstrated by that accomplishment. There may be more than one ECQ that fits for each accomplishment, as will likely be the case when you begin to match your ECQs. A suggested answer key is included below.

- **A. Leading Change:** Innovation, creativity, vision, strategic thinking
- **B. Leading People:** Conflict management, developing others, leveraging diversity
- **C. Results Driven:** Accountability, customer service, problem solving, technical credibility
- **D. Business Acumen:** Financial management, human capital management, technology management
- **E. Building Coalitions:** Partnering, political savvy, influencing, negotiating

Sample Top Ten List of Accomplishments

1. Supported the development and implementation of more than 10 disaster bills in the past 10 years. _____
2. Established a unit within a newly organized Department of Energy Office. _____
3. Led the "Requirements Documentation Team" of a significant A-76 study. _____
4. Answering the President's Management Agenda—built an E-gov for the Department. _____
5. Served as Vice President of the Hispanic Executives in Health and Science (HEES) Association. _____
6. Independently examined and determined need for coalition on training between Army and the Occupational Safety and Health Administration (OSHA). _____
7. In Japan, created "Big Brother/Big Sister" mentoring program in my department among Japanese local nationals, American soldiers, and civilian staff. _____
8. Led major rulemaking and changing of policies for hazardous waste and emergency response. _____
9. Served as technical expert to facilitate critical communications needs in support of Operation Liberty. _____
10. Created metrics system for accountability and submitted documentation to defend $26M budget requests from OMB. _____

Answer Key (Other answers may be possible)
1=A 2=C 3=E 4=D 5=B 6=E 7=B 8=A 9=A 10=D

Mapping Your Accomplishments to the ECQs

On the next two pages, you will practice mapping each of your top accomplishments to one of the five ECQs. Begin by creating a short outline of your top ten accomplishments in the space below. On the next page, mark the circles with the corresponding accomplishments that best demonstrate each of the five ECQs.

Some accomplishment examples can be matched to more than one ECQ. This flexibility will help you in your matching. However, if you do not have the right mix of accomplishments to cover the five ECQs, you can revise your accomplishment list to provide better examples for the required competencies.

Note: Your Top Ten List of Accomplishments does NOT have to be in order of importance.

My Top Ten List of Accomplishments Outline

1. _____

2. _____

3. _____

4. _____

5. _____

6. _____

7. _____

8. _____

9. _____

10. _____

If you do not have the right mix of accomplishments to cover the five ECQs, you can revise your accomplishment list to provide better examples for the required competencies.

Top Ten Accomplishments Map

In each circle, write a number from your Top Ten Accomplishments outline. Use the keyword list to decide where each accomplishment fits best.

ECQ 1: Leading Change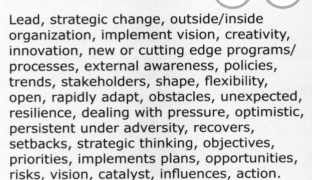

Lead, strategic change, outside/inside organization, implement vision, creativity, innovation, new or cutting edge programs/processes, external awareness, policies, trends, stakeholders, shape, flexibility, open, rapidly adapt, obstacles, unexpected, resilience, dealing with pressure, optimistic, persistent under adversity, recovers, setbacks, strategic thinking, objectives, priorities, implements plans, opportunities, risks, vision, catalyst, influences, action.

ECQ 2: Leading People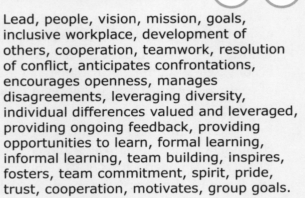

Lead, people, vision, mission, goals, inclusive workplace, development of others, cooperation, teamwork, resolution of conflict, anticipates confrontations, encourages openness, manages disagreements, leveraging diversity, individual differences valued and leveraged, providing ongoing feedback, providing opportunities to learn, formal learning, informal learning, team building, inspires, fosters, team commitment, spirit, pride, trust, cooperation, motivates, group goals.

ECQ 3: Results Driven

Meet organizational goals, customer expectations, make decisions, produce, results, apply technical knowledge, analyze problems, calculate risks, accountability, self and others, measurable, timely, cost-effective, determines objectives, priorities, delegates, accepts responsibility, complies with control systems, rules, customer service, internal/external customers, continuous improvement, commitment, effective, timely decisions, data, perceives impact, implications, entrepreneurship, positions organization, future success, identifies opportunities, builds, develops, improves, products and services, calculated risks, problem solving, identify, analyze, generate, evaluate, recommend, principles, procedures, requirements, regulations, policies.

ECQ 4: Business Acumen

Manage human capital, financial and information resources, understand financial processes, prepares, justifies, administers program budget, oversees procurement, contracting, achieve desired results, monitors expenditures, cost-benefit, sets priorities, builds, manages workforce, organizational goals, budget, staffing needs, recruit, select, appraise, reward, takes action, addresses performance problems, manages, multi-sector workforce, variety, up-to-date on technology, effective use of technology, ensures access to, security of technology.

ECQ 5: Building Coalitions

Build coalitions, internal, Joint, interagency, other federal agencies, state government, local government, nonprofit, private sector, multinational, foreign governments, international organizations, achieve common goals, partnering, develops, networks, alliances, collaborates across boundaries, build strategic relationships, political savvy, identifies internal/external politics, perceives organizational/political reality, influence, negotiate, persuade, build consensus, give and take, cooperation, obtain information, accomplish goals.

Sample Top Ten List of Accomplishments–Mapped

This sample Top Ten List of Accomplishments are started on pages 20-21 and expanded using the CCAR format on pages 32-34.

1. Conceived the idea, developed a vision and strategic plan, and stood up the Iraqi Republic Railway, which became the first government agency in Iraq to generate revenue and become self-sustaining, providing relief to logistical planning and response to all categories of contingency situations in that region. **(Building Coalitions)**

2. Provided planning and coordination guidance for military and DOD personnel and equipment for two joint federal and DOD emergency response exercises: SUDDEN RESPONSE (guided efforts of 143 emergency responders from NORTHCOM, FEMA and Region VII military personnel) and VIBRANT RESPONSE (a national training event involving 500+ DOD, federal, state and civilian emergency responders). **(Results Driven)**

3. Represented the Air Force and senior government officials before the Governor and other agencies, committees, organizations, media, unions, and private organizations. Developed and promoted relationships with federal and state military, and civilian and interagency organizations including FEMA and the state Emergency Manager and staff. Guided official staff in obtaining DOD Title 10 support as needed for disasters. Advised the Governor on the status of the federal response. **(Building Coalitions)**

4. Led the development of wilderness management plans for over 1.2 million acres of Congressionally designated wilderness through passage of two lands bills. **(Results Driven)**

5. Led comprehensive change in managing BLM's Land and Water Conservation Fund (LWCF) within the Department of the Interior (DOI) and the initiative to gain full funding for the LWCF Program, which required completely transforming how all four affected land management agencies work together. **(Leading Change)**

6. I reorganized the realty staff as part of an agency-wide transformation initiative designed to streamline staffing and identify opportunities to consolidate positions, especially in the Washington Office. In support of the Director, I recommended and implemented revisions to the organization that included eliminating certain positions, filling long vacant but vital positions, and utilizing alternative hiring authorities. My recommendations were incorporated into the transformed organization and approved by the agency's Executive Leadership Team. **(Business Acumen)**

7. I led a large organization with a budget of $100M, and 70 staff supporting 32,000 contracts throughout the Pacific region, reaching from Hawaii to Japan and satellite offices as far south as Australia, including the Pacific Headquarters. I introduced the concept of implementing Wide-Area Workflow (WAWF), a complete end-to-end processing of an invoice through to electronic payment, elevating the organization into the 21st century, by replacing antiquated technology and introducing automation that would create efficiencies enterprise-wide. After implementation interest penalty payments reduced 25% percent overall; invoice processing time initially reduced ~40% for contracts in the project. **(Business Acumen)**

8. The past couple years have been a time of enormous change in health care policy focused on the enactment of the Affordable Care Act (ACA). I facilitated health reform implementation efforts, and built and oversaw the policy coordination team necessary to meet the new health reform workload, as well as the ongoing workload of the agency to run Medicare, Medicaid and the Children's Health Insurance Program. **(Leading Change)**

9. I assumed leadership as the Acting Director of the Office of Strategic Operations and Regulatory Affairs, inheriting an organization ranked 21 of 22 offices, according to the annual Human Capital survey. Via team building and professional development, I am resolving some of the lingering conflict and continue to better utilize the office's human resources. The office is becoming more cohesive and better at meeting customer needs, which directly affects how policy from my organization will impact the public. My efforts led to a high-functioning team, enabling us to meet the Administration's priorities. Almost three years into the implementation effort, with ongoing demands on the team and other offices actively recruiting my staff, there has been low turnover. The team is well respected, with all staff performance far exceeding expectations. **(Leading People)**

10. I directed a large, multidisciplinary, international, and geographically dispersed staff across eight countries. I oversaw a diverse 120-person organization including local nationals, third-country nationals, contractors, government civilians, and military members located in several countries spread across 18 military installations supporting three Combatant Commands. This was a difficult position. This diversity caused cultural differences that I managed on a daily basis to balance the working environment across the larger staffs. **(Leading People)**

Chapter Four

Writing Your ECQs and TQs in the CCAR Model

SAMPLE SES ANNOUNCEMENT WITH KEYWORDS IN BOLD

Job Title: Director, Institutional Services
Department: Department Of Education
Agency: Office of Postsecondary Education

This position is located in the United States Department of Education, Office of Postsecondary Education (OPE), Higher Education Programs (HEP). The Director is responsible for the overall management of activities within the Office Institutional Services (IS). The Director plays a **critical leadership role** in advancing postsecondary education by working on a **national scale** to **improve the capacity and performance** of colleges and universities. The Director is responsible for the development of **annual funding requests**; recommending **program improvement strategies**, and oversight of the application and review process for all new and continuing programs administered by IS. The Director serves as **principle advisor** to the Deputy Assistant Secretary, HEP, OPE. The incumbent is responsible for the **formulation of policy, the design of operating programs, legislative recommendations, and the management of controversial and sensitive program-related issues in IS**.

The CCAR Model: Challenge | Context | Action | Result

OPM's recommended format for writing the Executive Core Qualifications is called the CCAR (Challenge, Context, Action, and Result) Model. Full ECQ essays must be in the CCAR format in order to be approved. The shorter mini-leadership bullets used in the five-page resume-based format may also be written in a summarized CCAR format, using some or all of the CCAR elements.

The Executive Resources Staff, rating and selecting officials, and Qualifications Review Board (QRB) members will be seeking specific information that validates a leadership story describing your achievements. You may also want to include professional and volunteer experience, education, training, and awards that demonstrate your leadership skills in a particular Executive Core Qualification (ECQ).

Developing an ECQ is much like writing any other essay. It has a brief summary introduction (the Challenge), a body (the Context and Action), and a conclusion (the Result).

Challenge: What was the specific problem that needed resolution? What made the achievement challenging? What were the sub-challenges that you faced?

- The challenges should describe a large-scope, organizational-level issue, with agency-wide, government-wide, or national/international effects or impacts.
- It should require more than individual actions and result in organizational impact.

Context: Define the factors (people, institutions, procedures) that made the challenge one of executive caliber. (Include dates, job title, and company name or project—the who, what, where, why, and when of the situation.)

- It should include redefinition of goals, changes in conditions, and some requirements to encourage other people or organizations to comply with your vision.
- Be specific in terms of factors that made the challenge substantial: resources, people, laws, regulations, deadlines, and complexity.

Action: What did you do that made a difference? What actions did you take?

- Express your achievement in a team environment, but focus on your role within the team.

Result: What difference did it make? Qualify and quantify results. Use numbers, dollar amounts, percentages. Use ripple effect examples (what other organizations did it reach or influence?).

- How did the accomplishment transform organizational performance? Metrics and quantifiable results are one of the most important components of ECQs.

Sample Top Ten List of Accomplishments–CCAR Version

We have taken five of the examples from the sample Top Ten List of Accomplishments on pages 20-21 and 28-29 and expanded the content using the CCAR format.

Top Ten CCAR Example #1

Challenge: The Iraqi Republic Railway was the first government agency in Iraq to generate revenue and with the potential to become self-sustaining but needed support.

Context: The railroad employed 11,000+ local nationals and needed assistance in the form of relief, logistical planning, and response to all categories of contingency situations in that region.

Actions: As the CEO-equivalent, I conceived the idea, developed a vision, and created a strategic plan to facilitate sensitive negotiations to reopen international trade routes and renegotiate previous contracts between internal and external agencies, customers and countries. Targeted and used the local sheikhs and pre-existing police force to protect the railroad against increasing armed attacks. Created a Task Force to sustain security and logistical operations. Briefed the U.S. Ambassador and Joint Commander in Theater and personally collaborated with senior Iraqi officials including the Ministry of Transportation, Ministry of Oil, Ministry of Trade, and Ministry of Defense.

Results: At the highest levels of government, led the creation of a logistics and distribution system and opened five distribution nodes in country, serving 150,000+ U.S. military and coalition forces with life support requirements.

Top Ten CCAR Example #2

Challenge: The coordination of federal emergency response in our area at the highest levels had been difficult due to varied regulations and differing opinions between the organizations.

Context: The emergency responders from FEMA and Region VII military personnel and NORTHCOM are responsible for all activities in North America, Canada and Mexico for active duty Soldiers and including the Joint Task Force (JTF) headquarters, collocated with the FEMA Regional Response Coordination Center.

Actions: Provided planning and coordination guidance for military and DOD personnel and equipment for two joint federal and DOD emergency response exercises: SUDDEN RESPONSE (guided efforts of 143 emergency responders from NORTHCOM, FEMA and Region VII military personnel) and VIBRANT RESPONSE (a national training event involving 500+ DOD, federal, state and civilian emergency responders). This was a key staff exercise where we tested the skills of key DOD planners.

Results: All participants developed the process of coordinating with upper level IGO/NGO departments and prepared for real-world disasters.

Top Ten CCAR Example #3

Challenge: Federal emergency response in our area needed critical coordination with state activities to maximize the resources available at the state level during disasters.

Context: I represented the Air Force and senior government officials before the Governor and other agencies, committees, organizations, media, unions, and private organizations.

Actions: Updated and provided situational assessments to the Governor and communicated with the State Director of Emergency Management, the State Emergency Operations Center (EOC), the FEMA Regional Response Coordination Center (RRCC), members of National Incident Management Assistance Teams (IMAT), the National Response Coordination Center (NRCC), and other officials, as necessary. Navigated contentious turf battles. Developed and promoted relationships with federal and state military, and civilian and interagency organizations including FEMA and the State Emergency Manager and staff. Guided official staff in obtaining DOD Title 10 support as needed for disasters. Advised the Governor on the status of the federal response.

Results: Planned, coordinated, and integrated Defense Support for Civil Authorities with the Region VII Defense Coordinating Officer, Governor, Adjutant General (TAG), local, state, and Federal agencies (Department of Homeland Security, Department of Transportation, others), primarily within the region, and as needed within Federal Emergency Management Agency (FEMA) Region VII. Effectively managed several major disasters via the partnerships.

Top Ten CCAR Example #4

Challenge: With the passage of two land bills by Congress the District had over 1.2 million acres of new wilderness identified in 20 separate wilderness areas. One of the requirements for management of wilderness is the development of a specific wilderness management plan for each area designated. The District had no experience with wilderness management and our staff had a huge learning curve.

Context: As the Region Director, I led the development of wilderness management plans for over 1.2 million acres of Congressionally designated wilderness through passage of two lands bills.

Actions: I led a push by the District and Field Offices to compete for increased funding. This funding was necessary to hire and train additional staff. Another aspect of this process was ensuring we provided consistent outreach to the local government officials on the progress we were making. This outreach also was an opportunity to ensure these local governments were given the chance to provide their perspective on wilderness management.

Results: Before my departure from the District we had successfully completed 12 wilderness plans. These plans were complex plans that set the guidelines for management of the wilderness areas. These completed plans were also readily accepted by the local governments and the constituents who used these areas.

Top Ten CCAR Example #5

Challenge: The Bureau of Land Mangement's (BLM'S) Land and Water Conservation Fund (LWCF) receives $900 million a year from offshore energy royalties. However, Congressional appropriators have consistently withheld much of that money to fund other federal priorities. My challenge included meeting both Administration and Congressional expectations for a more robust and transparent collaborative LWCF process, justifying increased LWCF funding to stakeholders, while working with the three other federal agencies to set common goals and processes, and track the resource benefits of an increased number of land acquisitions within the BLM.

Context: In my role as Director, I led comprehensive change in managing LWCF within the Department of the Interior (DOI) and the initiative to gain full funding for the LWCF Program, which required completely transforming how all four affected land management agencies work together.

Actions: I designed a collaborative funding scenario and introduced a completely new model for shared efforts across the four federal land management agencies, all DOI agencies, and the U.S. Forest Service (USFS). Leading this group of senior leaders, we prioritized the public lands into six priority landscapes where all agencies were involved in conservation initiatives. I asked the members to relook at the importance of the landscapes; and we developed new criteria for how land acquisition projects would rank, enhancing consideration for individual regional priorities to ensure the program reflected ground-level perspectives and needs from the user groups.

Results: This new process vetted by the Secretaries of Interior and Agriculture resulted in a first-ever collaborative, landscape-level submission of land acquisition projects from the four land management agencies for submission to Congress. The new process gained widespread support from within the agencies and across the Departments, Congressional staff, conservation partners, and OMB, and as a result, the President's budget request reflected this increased support. Historically, these agencies had never talked together before, and I introduced them to a model that they all brought into the future—I pulled the missions of four different agencies under one umbrella to achieve conservation goals at a landscape level.

REMINDER: These accomplishments are not bragging. They are statements that describe how you have provided effective leadership. What have you done as a leader, manager, innovator in your organization to improve or change or transform operations; save or increase funding; improve information management; restructure or improve the workforce and enhance performance; develop and motivate your employees; be decisive in problem-solving; and otherwise make a difference?

Keywords

As you already know, it is much easier to verify qualification for a position if the resume and the ECQs have the correct keywords for the position.

As you craft your ECQs and executive resume, find the keywords in the:

- **Vacancy Announcement:** Find the keywords in the Duties, Qualifications, Specialized Experience, and Questionnaire sections. See examples with the keywords highlighted below and on pages 30 and 132.

- **28 Leadership Competencies:** These keywords are presented on the pages 36-45 with the definitions of the ECQs and Leadership Competencies.

Keywords from Vacancy Announcements (Keywords in bold)

Job Title: SUPERINTENDENT, MARINE METEOROLOGY DIVISION
Department: Department of the Navy
Agency: Office of Naval Research, Naval Research Laboratory

As Superintendent of the Marine Meteorology Division, you will provide **executive direction and technical leadership in the development of policies and objectives** necessary in conducting a program of **research, development, and application-oriented activities in the analysis** and **prediction of meteorological processes** throughout the depth of the atmosphere and as part of the coupled air/ocean/land system. The Superintendent is responsible for the **overall planning and direction of a coordinated research and development program** in **meteorology and atmospheric sciences** designed to meet the present and future needs of the Navy.

Job Title: Director, Executive Services Directorate
Department: Department of Defense
Agency: Washington Headquarters Services

With a workforce of over 2,500 civilian, military, and contractors organized into 11 directorates and offices, Washington Headquarters Services (WHS) personnel contribute to the mission of our Defense customers by managing DoD-wide programs and operations for the Pentagon Reservation and DOD leased facilities in the National Capital Region.

This position is in the Senior Executive Service (SES), a small elite group of top government leaders. SES members possess a diverse portfolio of experiences including **strong skills to lead across organizations**. As a Senior Executive, you will influence the direction of **innovation and transformation of the federal government** and **lead** the next generation of public servants.

As the Director, Executive Services Directorate (ESD), you will provide a **broad spectrum of executive and administrative services** to the Secretary of Defense, Deputy Secretary of Defense, and their immediate staffs.

ECQ Insights | ECQ 1–Leading Change

Definition: The ability to develop and implement an organizational vision, which integrates key national and program goals, priorities, values, and other factors. Inherent to it is the ability to balance change and continuity—to continually strive to improve customer service and program performance within the basic government framework, to create a work environment that encourages creative thinking, and to maintain focus, intensity, and persistence, even under adversity.

Leadership Competencies

Creativity and Innovation: Develops new insights into situations; questions conventional approaches; encourages new ideas and innovations; designs and implements new or cutting-edge programs/processes.

External Awareness: Understands and keeps up-to-date on local, national, and international policies and trends that affect the organization and shape stakeholders' views; is aware of the organization's impact on the external environment.

Flexibility: Is open to change and new information; rapidly adapts to new information, changing conditions, or unexpected obstacles.

Resilience: Deals effectively with pressure; remains optimistic and persistent, even under adversity. Recovers quickly from setbacks.

Strategic Thinking: Formulates objectives and priorities, and implements plans consistent with long-term interests of the organization in a global environment. Capitalizes on opportunities; manages risks.

Vision: Takes a long-term view and builds a shared vision with others; acts as a catalyst for organizational change. Influences others to translate vision into action.

Writer's Insight

In reviewing the competencies for Leading Change, the definitions clearly reveal that this ECQ is about successfully leading organizational change—it should not be narrow in scope, and it truly needs to focus on "leading change," as opposed to "creating results."

For example, Service Motivation (or customer service) indicates a significant paradigm change for some agencies. Applicants should develop an example in which they have led or significantly contributed to a change in the organization resulting in improved customer service.

Additionally, it is important to tie ECQ responses to current government initiatives. You can easily tie strategic thinking and vision to changing an organization's approach to internal and external customers; this would be considered an example that demonstrates executive level experience. Then, you can tie it to continual learning, since you have learned much about change, and about ways and means to effect change to improve customer service.

CCAR Template

Challenge: What was the organizational change you were trying to lead or direct? What challenges did you overcome?

Context: What were the issues surrounding the change—what barriers were in place to prevent successful change? Who, what, why, when, and where?

Action: What steps did you take personally to lead or effect the change?

Result: What measurable results were achieved? How did you measure them, and how were they recognized? What was the bottom-line change to organizational performance internally and across boundaries?

Example of ECQ Template

Challenge: Changes in management, lack of program commitment, lack of communication, reduced resources, and conflicting priorities.

Context: Within Department of Commerce, program management of energy program had been matrixed with other programs; organization not focused on meeting requirements, old IG findings not taken care of, and lack of program management and direction causing problems with public and other federal agencies.

Action: Developed plan of action and work team to identify issues, prioritize program development and remediation, and develop metrics to measure results.

Result: Program turnaround and improvement, adding value to Department of Commerce and improving public relationships.

KEYWORDS

lead

strategic change

outside/inside organization

implement vision

creativity

innovation

new or cutting edge programs/processes

external awareness

policies

trends

stakeholders

shape

flexibility

open

rapidly adapt

obstacles

unexpected

resilience

dealing with pressure

optimistic

persistent under adversity

recovers

setbacks

strategic thinking

objectives

priorities

implements plans

opportunities

risks

vision

catalyst

ECQ Insights | ECQ 2–Leading People

Definition: The ability to design and implement strategies that maximize employee potential and foster high ethical standards in meeting the organization's vision, mission, and goals.

Leadership Competencies

Conflict Management: Encourages creative tension and differences of opinions. Anticipates and takes steps to prevent counter-productive confrontations. Manages and resolves conflicts and disagreements in a constructive manner.

Leveraging Diversity: Fosters an inclusive workplace where diversity and individual differences are valued and leveraged to achieve the vision and mission of the organization.

Developing Others: Develops the ability of others to perform and contribute to the organization by providing ongoing feedback and by providing opportunities to learn through formal and informal methods.

Team Building: Inspires and fosters team commitment, spirit, pride, and trust. Facilitates cooperation and motivates team members to accomplish group goals.

Writer's Insight

When developing a response to Leading People, take a moment to reflect on the Leading People competencies.

As you read the leadership competencies, note that each of the leadership competencies highlights the personal actions taken by the applicant—not the actions taken by staff, or through others. The ECQs should focus on your personal contributions that demonstrate how you lead people.

- In leading people, have you coached or mentored?
- What success have you had in the placement and retention of diverse applicants?
- How have you successfully managed conflict in your organization, and what was the organizational effect?

CCAR Template

Challenge: What was the challenge of leading people in this accomplishment/project? What issues did you overcome? Describe the conflict.

Context: Describe your organization and the diversity of your staff.

Action: What actions did you take to lead people through the challenges and to achieve positive change or reach results? Or, HOW did you lead people in this project?

Result: Describe your leadership skills and the results to the larger organization that were achieved by rallying people to follow your vision and meet organizational milestones.

Example of ECQ Template

Challenge: Newly appointed manager of organization with significant issues regarding performance and direction.

Context: Within the Department of Commerce, a decision had been made to "right size" the organization. I came into the position just after actions were completed, and I was faced with meeting organizational goals and objectives with a demoralized workforce.

Action: Met with employees, enhanced listening, did not over-commit to resolve problems, discussed need to move past organizational issues and improve customer service.

Result: Met 100% of organizational goals and, according to an internal survey, increased work satisfaction for nearly three-quarters of the staff.

KEYWORDS

lead
people
vision
mission
goals
inclusive workplace
development of others
cooperation
teamwork
resolution of conflict
anticipates confrontations
encourages openness
manages disagreements
leveraging diversity
individual differences valued and leveraged
providing ongoing feedback
providing opportunities to learn
formal learning
informal learning
team building
inspires
fosters
team commitment
spirit
pride
trust
cooperation
motivates
group goals

ECQ Insights | ECQ 3–Results Driven

Definition: The ability to make timely and effective decisions and produce results through strategic planning and the implementation and evaluation of programs and policies. This core qualification stresses accountability and continuous improvement.

Leadership Competencies

Accountability: Holds self and others accountable for measurable high-quality, timely, and cost-effective results. Determines objectives, sets priorities, and delegates work. Accepts responsibility for mistakes. Complies with established control systems and rules.

Customer Service: Anticipates and meets the needs of both internal and external customers. Delivers high-quality products and services; is committed to continuous improvement.

Decisiveness: Makes well-informed, effective, and timely decisions, even when data are limited or solutions produce unpleasant consequences; perceives the impact and implications of decisions.

Entrepreneurship: Positions the organization for future success by identifying new opportunities; builds the organization by developing or improving products or services. Takes calculated risks to accomplish organizational objectives.

Problem Solving: Identifies and analyzes problems; weighs relevance and accuracy of information; generates and evaluates alternative solutions; makes recommendations.

Technical Credibility: Understands and appropriately applies principles, procedures, requirements, regulations, and policies related to specialized expertise.

Writer's Insight

In responding to Results Driven, describe a management or leadership situation demonstrating personal accountability and commitment to achieving far-reaching results.

In reviewing your work or volunteer experience, select an example where you were challenged to improve customer service, explaining how you used your problem-solving abilities to develop a solution and the decisions you made throughout the process (including those that were unpopular).

Address your technical credibility by demonstrating your ability to achieve results in a large organization or corporation by guiding programs and transformations through administrative and other processes, which may often represent significant challenges in achieving results.

CCAR Template

Challenge: What challenges did you face? What was the condition of the environment that needed changing? What did you identify as needing improvements or overhaul?

Context: Describe the dates, job title, and company name or project—the who, what, where, why, and when of the situation.

Action: What steps did you take personally to achieve results? Use "I" with Actions. Who did you collaborate with?

Result: What measurable results were achieved—how did you measure them, and how were they recognized? Give metrics if possible.

Example of ECQ Template

Challenge: Serious issue in Real Estate Division regarding use and application of professional design services used by the Department of Commerce.

Context: Use of architectural/engineering firms causing problems in costs, use of resources and ability to manage construction, not using advanced building technologies.

Action: Took steps to educate senior management on need for practice changes, benchmarked, and developed action plan to incorporate changes into new building approval process.

Result: Program turnaround and improvement, adding value to Department of Commerce, and improved results, saving the Department millions of dollars.

KEYWORDS

meet organizational goals
customer expectations
make decisions
produce
results
apply technical knowledge
analyze problems
calculate risks
accountability
self and others
measurable
timely
cost-effective
determines objectives
priorities
delegates
accepts responsibility
complies with control systems
customer service
internal/external customers
continuous improvement
commitment
effective
identify | analyze
generate | evaluate
recommend
principles | procedures
requirements | regulations
timely decisions
data | rules
perceives impact
implications
entrepreneurship
positions organization
future success
identifies opportunities
builds | develops
improves
products and services
calculated risks
problem solving

ECQ Insights | ECQ 4–Business Acumen

Definition: The ability to acquire and administer human, financial, material, and information resources in a manner that instills public trust and accomplishes the organization's mission, and the ability to use new technology to enhance decision-making.

Leadership Competencies

Financial Management: Understands the organization's financial processes. Prepares, justifies, and administers the program budget. Oversees procurement and contracting to achieve desired results. Monitors expenditures and uses cost-benefit thinking to set priorities.

Human Capital Management: Builds and manages the workforce based on organizational goals, budget considerations, and staffing needs. Ensures that employees are appropriately recruited, selected, appraised, and rewarded; takes action to address performance problems. Manages a multi-sector workforce and a variety of work situations.

Technology Management: Keeps up-to-date on technological developments. Makes effective use of technology to achieve results. Ensures access to and security of technology systems.

Writer's Insight

Business Acumen is typically one of the most difficult ECQs to write. The ECQ is very broad, and asks for examples across all aspects of business focusing on Financial Management, Human Capital Management, and Technology Management. The best way to approach this ECQ may be to identify two or three shorter examples.

Focus on examples describing a management or leadership situation where you demonstrated leadership in at least two of the three required leadership competencies.

For example, you may have provided leadership and direction in the automation of an agency-level process or procedure.

You may have managed large-scale budgets, in which you were responsible for successful formulation and execution, but you have had to defend requested increases or develop a plan of action when funding levels were not approved.

You may have participated in the development or assessment of human resources tools, such as a new performance evaluation system or other HR tools.

CCAR Template

Challenge: What was the challenge of this business, information technology, or human capital situation, problem, or need? What challenge did you face for the operations or administration of a major program?

Context: Describe the situational background and provide an introductory or overview statement of your ability to manage funds and staffing needs, and to integrate technology into the workplace to create organizational efficiencies.

Action: What steps did you take personally to manage this IT, finance, or human resources challenge, project, or change?

Result: Describe the organizational impact. If the example focuses on finances, then describe in quantifiable results the changes you delivered in terms of saving dollars or restructuring budgets; if the example focuses on human capital/staff, then describe what system you designed to create a strong workforce; and if the example focuses on technology integration, then describe the results of streamlined operations due to the introduction of automation.

Example of ECQ Template

Challenge: Organization required leadership in use of information technology and disposal of 1,000 buildings.

Context: Organization lacked plan of action to effect change in these areas.

Action: Worked with technical staff and senior management to obtain support for changes, and obtained additional funding and resources required to make changes.

Result: Improved use of agency resources and programs, including streamlining operations and gaining efficiencies based on use of automation.

KEYWORDS

human capital

information resources

understand financial processes

justifies

administers program budget

oversees procurement

contracting

achieve desired results

monitors expenditures

cost-benefit

sets priorities

builds

manages workforce

organizational goals

budget

staffing needs

recruit

select

appraise

reward

addresses performance problems

multi-sector workforce

variety

up-to-date on technology

effective use of technology

ensures access to

security of technology

social media

e-gov

virtual

cyber

telework

databases

ECQ Insights | ECQ 5–Building Coalitions

Definition: The ability to build coalitions internally and with other federal agencies, state and local governments, nonprofit and private sector organizations, foreign governments, or international organizations to achieve common goals.

Leadership Competencies

Partnering: Develops networks and builds alliances; collaborates across boundaries to build strategic relationships and achieve common goals.

Political Savvy: Identifies the internal and external politics that impact the work of the organization. Perceives organizational and political reality and acts accordingly.

Influencing/Negotiating: Persuades others; builds consensus through give and take; gains cooperation from others to obtain information and accomplish goals.

Writer's Insight

The key to this ECQ is the effective development of partnerships and management of key negotiations in support of agency goals and objectives.

OPM is looking for experience in developing and maintaining effective cross-agency, inter-governmental, multi-national, and industry (contractors and academia) relationships to form coalitions and partners that facilitate the greater efficiency, effectiveness, or customer service of the government and to form joint capabilities and information sharing across the globe.

Aim for examples of building coalitions that have stood the test of time. Examples like facilitating or planning an event are usually the least successful.
- Have you built an inter-agency organization?
- Did you cross over agency lines, or reach out to private industry, in order to accomplish a goal or mission?
- How have you improved your organization's performance by working with others?
- Did you lead a group that successfully passed a bill, or have you worked closely with Congress?

CCAR Template

Challenge: What was the challenge of a Building Coalitions situation? Bringing people together often creates divergent viewpoints. What areas needed to be negotiated?

Context: Describe the members (senior leaders by title or organization), the agencies or entities (government agencies, industry, foreign national organizations) of the coalition, and your role within the coalition (leader, member, and contributor). Describe the purpose or need for the coalition. Describe the location (USA, other country, other military service, etc.), and the significance of that.

Action: What actions did you take to build the coalition? Describe your ability to negotiate, influence, or persuade.

Result: What was the result or outcome of the coalition's efforts? Was there a continuing coalition? Describe improved relationships and collaboration.

Example of ECQ Template

Challenge: Limited local infrastructure, no local trust of government or large business institutions, no effective banking system, and obstructionist elements of Iraqi society.

Context: Initiated improvements in the economic situation in Iraq. The objective was to use our contracts to offer business opportunities to the local population.

Action: Held an industry day in the international zone. Coordinated with the U.S. and Iraqi security forces to ensure a safe venue. Partnered with installation leadership to increase the size of a small shopping area that already existed on a base. Arranged a cross-functional team (my staff, the Iraqi government, intelligence and operations officers and security personnel) to begin the process of increasing the Iraqi vendor base.

Result: Developed local small businesses, and built "safe haven" economic zones that resulted in a threefold increase, from 25% to 75%, of contract awards to local Iraqi vendors within six months. Met the strategic regional objectives of improving the Iraqi economy, creating jobs for Iraqi men and women, increasing goodwill, and deterring extremism.

KEYWORDS

build coalitions
internal
other federal agencies
state government
local government
nonprofit
private sector
joint
interagency
multinational
foreign governments
international organizations
achieve common goals
partnering
develops
networks
alliances
collaborates across boundaries
build strategic relationships
political saavy
identifies internal/external politics
perceives organizational/ political reality
influence
negotiate
persuade
build consensus
give and take
cooperation
obtain information
accomplish goals
politically sensitive
debate

Sample ECQ Essays

The following ECQ essays are from real case files of The Resume Place (names, locations, and dates have been fictionalized to protect client identities). Some examples include the "before" and "after." As an exercise, review and evaluate each example, identify the problems with each, and examine how those problems were resolved in the final document.

The ECQ essays in this book are one page each. In 12-point font with one-inch margins, that equals about 3,200 characters or a bit less than 500 words. By contrast, two-page ECQ essays can be 4,500 to a maximum of 8,000 characters for various federal online application systems (or two pages maximum for hard copy submissions). Applicants should always be mindful of the specific requirements for different agencies or federal application job boards, as responses/ECQ essays can range from 250 characters to 8,000 characters. You should have a variety of story lengths available for specific job announcements and application types. The CCAR element labels (Challenge, Context, etc.) in these examples are for reference only and should not be included in final essays.

Chapter 7 of this book contains shortened versions of these ECQs for use in the five-page resume-based application format, ranging from about 50 words to 150 words (about 300 to 1,000 characters).

> Even if the announcement indicates that an applicant can use up to 8,000 characters, a shorter and more concise essay response, with powerful, clear writing, is often more attractive to the readers/reviewers than a long, jumbled essay.

Leading Change
1. Delta Air Lines Turnaround Story – Before and After
2. Economic Transformation in Iraq – After only

Leading People
3. Employee Buy-In for Performance Improvement – Before and After
4. Low Team Morale – After only

Results Driven
5. Created a New Organizational Strategy for Agency – Before and After
6. Created Profitable Operations – After only

Business Acumen
7. Secured Location for University-Hosted National Center – Before and After
8. NSPS – After only

Building Coalitions
9. Missile Defense Coalitions – Before and After
10. Audit Coalition – After only

Technical Qualification Samples (3)

ECQ #1: Leading Change

Tip: Leading Change is about the ability to create and manage multi-agency changes and innovation, which meet the goals, priorities, and values of the organization; it also involves responding to pressure and being flexible under changing conditions. Use a strong opening paragraph that indicates you are in the midst of a big change, without a clear direction for where to go next. Be sure to include "before and after" facts.

Leading Change ECQ Example 1

Delta Air Lines Turnaround Story (Private Industry to SES)

▶ Before

Elected and served as Delta Air Lines' Chief Information Officer and Managing Director Information Technologies. Led corporate critical division of 1,900 technical professionals organized in two diverse partially owned subsidiaries and an internal department. Working with a mandate to fix past problems with corporate technology, I established and enriched relationships with key users across the company to build plan of action and time frame for the transformation. Results began immediately with significant improvement in the operational efficiency and reliability of the airlines global infrastructure, which provided for greatly improved customer service at airports and reservations offices throughout the world. Additionally, critical applications projects were completed on time and within budget resulting in corporate cost savings and revenue goals being attained. The technology budget was increased during my tenure from $350m to over $550m.

What is wrong with the above essay? Check all that apply

❑ Too short

❑ Does not cover the CCAR format

❑ Misses the Leading Change competency definition

▶ After

(Challenge) As Delta's Chief Information Officer (CIO), I inherited an established division with an operating plan that only covered the next six months of activities. Responsible for Delta's worldwide technology management, I realized that this short-term planning was insufficient for creating value for our stakeholders.

(Context) Since Delta's planning process was only short term, general in nature, only identified operating expenses and funding for small-scale projects, and capital spending projects were not included and were funded on an "as-needed" basis, I correctly assumed that other operating divisions faced similar challenges. It was evident the company needed to develop a strategic planning process that would address short- and long-term planning, and effectively forecast capital and other expenditures.

(Action) As an executive passionately committed to leading change resulting in improved organizational performance, My vision was to create a long-term strategy that would stretch the corporate view of the future to a three-year horizon.

I succeeded in guiding multiple transformational initiatives for Delta Air Lines. For the IT division, my expectation was simple: create a plan to which people and financial resources could be committed in order to carry out the business objectives of the airline. With 1,900 people in my division and $350M in planned expenditures, I needed to ensure that the IT organization and Delta had engaged in a thoughtful, future-focused process, to ensure that we had identified key strategic and operational objectives, and within that strategy, to ensure effective forecasting and resourcing of projects to enhance our business objectives.

To address this strategic gap, I met one-on-one with my executive peers, which led to a group recommendation to the Chief Executive Officer (CEO) and executive operating council, gaining approval to create the first draft of Delta's strategic operating plan. Technology would be a key driver in the strategy development, based on the potential for efficiencies, the need to deliver on new initiatives to drive revenues, or to achieve cost containment. With approval in place, I wanted to exploit our opportunity for change, and led efforts to the effective design of a strategic planning process. Plan development included the creation and use of a corporate dashboard and metrics. Working with my executive peers, I led the development of and presented the first draft to the operating and executive councils, where we received "hands-down" approval to integrate the strategic planning process as a critical element of the Delta planning regimen.

(Result) I led the development and execution of the first Delta strategic operating plan. Plan development and implementation were integrated into the Delta planning process, providing a consistent process to measure organizational performance and success. The planning process allowed Delta to allocate resources effectively. Initially capital spending dropped by 25%; and use of the strategic planning process allowed Delta to effectively continue to increase its capital spending program, which reached $1.5B.

Leading Change ECQ Example 2

Economic Transformation in Iraq (Military Officer to SES)

▶ After Only

(Challenge) When deployed to Iraq as the Director for Contracting-Forces, subordinate to Joint Contracting Command-Iraq/Afghanistan, I provided overarching leadership for contracting support for 140,000 troops and 12 Regional Contracting Centers, stationed in Iraq and Afghanistan, and executive oversight for more than 5,000 contracts worth $550M, for work including construction, vehicle maintenance, intelligence gathering, media services, and water bottling. Shortly after my arrival, the leader of Multi-National Forces Iraq challenged my organization to take on a more strategic focus; specifically to focus on his strategic objective of improving the Iraqi economy. I accepted the challenge of meeting this objective, but my organization was not immediately ready.

(Context) My 12 regional centers, while operating well, were largely operating independently of each other, without any integrated focus or standardized procedures—capabilities critical to successful strategic operations. My vision was to create an organization capable of taking on and achieving strategic Theater objectives, while still supporting tactical operations. To realize this vision, I faced numerous obstacles to effecting major organizational changes in an environment of perverse violence and extreme fluidity. The challenges included making changes to operational focus, creating capacity in the organization to take on increased work, developing common processes, and introducing infrastructure changes across the enterprise.

(Action) Time was of the essence; I took decisive action to implement the change. To begin, I challenged my staff to develop an action plan. I then revisited many military combat leaders to explain the changes about to happen. This critical step provided them situational awareness, engendered trust, and obtained their buy-in. I focused the center leaders on the need to standardize processes. I was honest and direct, telling them that the integrity and credibility of deployed procurement operations was on the line; that Congress and the public questioned our ability to make quality business decisions, while still supporting our mission. We agreed to establish a new quality review process to ensure all products met standard.

(Result) My leadership inspired innovative and creative thinking among my management team. Before introduction of my changes, the organization was not capable of supporting broader strategic initiatives and economic development faltered; after the shift in operations and workloads across the regional centers, we began effectively executing procurement programs to improve/speed the process of economic recovery in Iraq and Afghanistan. Dialogue I engaged in with senior leaders throughout Iraq and Afghanistan, began focusing on both supporting the troops AND strategic economic development. This shift in primary focus completely revamped my organization's role in the region—I began supporting nation building; we addressed NATO issues, grew infrastructure, designated economic safe zones, and built trust amongst the Iraqi business people and public. Overall, I led my organization in delivering a wider range of services, with much broader impact—at the national level, and transformed a tactical operation into a strategic powerhouse.

ECQ #2: Leading People

Tip: Diversity encompasses managing and leading a variety of differences in staff from varying levels of seniority (junior level to senior level/no degree to multiple degrees); a mixture of personnel from various backgrounds and organizations (military, federal, contractors, foreign nationals, expats, industry); age differences (Gen X/Y/Millennials working with Baby Boomers); and varied skill sets (multi-functional teams—from engineers to finance specialists, and skilled/vocational to professionals and credentialed employees) working on the same project. A strong leader of people is capable of motivating teams and managing internal and external stakeholders across industries, disciplines and cultures—in matrix and other organizational structures.

Leading People ECQ Example 1
Employee Buy-In for Performance Improvement (DoD Contractor)

▶ Before

When I began my tenure at DOE in November 2010, the client was extremely dissatisfied with the performance of my predecessor and the existing team. Client satisfaction ratings at that time were 1.0 on a 4.0 scale. Several critical cyber security initiatives were on hold or not bearing fruit for the department, and the CISO and Deputy CISO were not happy with the contractor management. My challenge was to assess the situation, identify the reasons for failure, and quickly implement the necessary changes to get this critical program on track. I spoke with every member of the client and contractor teams in my first two weeks and recognized almost immediately that the majority of the contractor workforce at that time was not aware of the organization big-picture goals and that communication among teams was sorely lacking. Poor communications had created a culture that lacked vision and an understanding of how daily work tied into the client's objectives for the departmental cyber security program.

Lack of sound management discipline and a serious lack of the appropriate cyber security skill sets were also the cause of project failure and client dissatisfaction. Upon concluding my initial assessment, I took decisive and immediate action to rectify these deficiencies. Everyone was given an opportunity to perform, and if they were incapable or unwilling to do so, they were moved from the program to other projects. In less than one year, three senior managers and more than ten cyber staff were removed and replaced with high-performing, highly skilled personnel. Within three months of hire, I was recognized by leadership for my efforts at transforming the cyber security team by being promoted from Director of Cyber Security to Associate Vice President with direct reporting responsibility to the Senior VP of Operations, a move that provided me with nearly autonomous control over the cyber contractor program. During these first crucial months, my managers and I were engaged in a complete transformation of our workforce to lead and motivate them to achieve the mission and goals of the Office of the ACIO for Cyber Security by providing staff with opportunities for personal and professional development through the funding and provision of technical and management training and incentives for academic achievements and earning cyber security certifications. We created a culture where employees were valued. This effort to shift the focus to results orientation and build a culture of trust and cooperation among the contractor team produced immediate benefits for our client. Results included:

- Improved communications and reporting, regular meetings among feds and contractors
- Took direct involvement in the management of budgets and resource allocation for all projects
- At the same time providing strategic guidance to the client, I ensured that this strategic vision was communicated to all levels of my staff to include them on the big-picture to motivate them to execute their missions

What is wrong with the above essay? Check all that apply:

❏ Does not meet the definition of Leading People

❏ Bullets and not full paragraphs / narrative writing style

❏ Does not cover leadership

❏ Not in the CCAR format

To make this narrative more effective, we needed to show how the applicant went above and beyond in leading people to meet the mission. See the rewrite on the next page.

▶ After

(Challenge) When I began my tenure at DOE, the client was extremely displeased with the performance of my predecessor and the existing team. Client satisfaction ratings were at an all time low (1.0/4.0 scale). Several critical cyber security initiatives were on hold and the Chief Information Security Officer (CISO) and Deputy CISO were dissatisfied with the contractor management. My challenge was to turn around this underperforming organization and put this critical program on track.

(Context) I employ a strategic human resources leadership approach in managing a workforce to achieve maximum growth, productivity, job satisfaction, and a quality work environment, and I inspire people to embrace change. My leadership of the contractor change initiative required employee "buy-in" to maximize the potential for successful performance improvement. While I could have simply said, "This is the direction we are going," I wanted this change management process to be different, where staff were inspired by the possibilities offered in the change, recognized the organizational and personal benefits, and were active participants in the process—rather than being "led" through the process. With my innovative leadership, we could engage in a change process where ideas were valued, and staff were motivated to surface their own ideas for change, resulting in a collaborative transformational process that would benefit all staff involved in the change.

(Action) To achieve this goal, I designed a variety of employee engagement forums to share my vision, and led discussions with large and small groups and individuals, seeking ideas for change, commitment and opportunities to promote inclusion and participation. Using this approach, and conducting these forums in a collaborative manner, I was successful in opening communication channels and establishing a continuing dialogue on change management, functional suggestions and opportunities. Within this environment, the staff and I worked together to openly evaluate the "value add" of change suggestions, and determine which ideas were practical and executable. Some of the dialogue was challenging. I applied sensitivity in addressing past performance; however, I was able to manage these conversations effectively, addressing conflict at the earliest stage, without impact to our process. These conversations became a foundational element of our change and contributed significantly to accelerate the change management process, meeting DOE requirements with increasing effectiveness.

(Result) Because of my leadership and willingness to address these issues directly, after several months, attitudes began to change; staff began to work together and challenge one another to excel. This change resulted in timely completion of projects, tripling of customer satisfaction ratings, and recognition of the team's positive attitude by other managers. I wanted to ensure that these changes were effectively recognized, implementing a new focus on award and recognition for teamwork, knowledge sharing, and improved customer service. I highlighted teamwork in meetings and with customers. Overall, my leadership has resulted in improved staff performance, customer service, morale, and long-term retention.

Leading People ECQ Example 2

Low Team Morale (Industry to SES)

▶ After Only

(**Challenge**) In my most recent assignment as Executive Vice President of Consumer Goods USA in Long Beach, California, my headquarters' staff was composed of personnel from two US regions, the Headquarters, and members from two countries. This comprised the management team and the mid-level staff. I quickly recognized that the management team handled their direct-reports in a very hierarchical, depreciative manner, manifested in a chasm between the management team decision-makers and the mid-level staff. This resulted in low morale, self-esteem and motivation on the part of the middle management staff, accompanied by a very high level of complaints and personnel turbulence.

(**Context**) I, at the same time, recognized in my mid-level staff much talent and potential. With the amount of work and challenges in the current business across the USA and in five other countries, plus my intent to quickly enter other unexploited markets; combined with a need to support the integration into our business of a newly acquired and refurbished plant, I urgently needed to unlock the potential of my mid-level staff and give them autonomy to perform to their potential. I also needed to impose my will on the current management team, to demonstrate to them the benefits of a more enlightened, inclusive approach to managing their people, yet at the same time not alienate them and thus lose sorely needed momentum in our business operations.

(**Action**) I accomplished this by officially establishing a "leadership team" composed of the management team and their direct-report mid-level managers. I officially inducted the new members of the leadership team and briefed them on their duties and obligations as leaders in our company. They attended my periodic management team meetings. The new members participated enthusiastically, taking the initiative and offering sound proposals to business issues, volunteering to lead projects and otherwise demonstrating that they were indeed leaders.

(**Result**) We were now addressing more issues and projects simultaneously than previously. The morale of my new leaders improved noticeably, and this enthusiasm cascaded to the entire organization. My management team welcomed the increased momentum in the organization and increasingly trusted and empowered their staffs. I reinforced my new leaders' role and my trust in them by direct personal contact without having to directly involve their management team supervisors.

To capitalize on my initial success and to fully establish the new leadership team, I scheduled an off-site meeting three months later to inaugurate the upcoming annual and strategic planning process. I directed that the meeting be prepared and conducted by the new leadership team members, who presented the current business status and their proposals to the management team. This extremely successful meeting fully institutionalized the new leadership construct. I smoothly achieved a fundamental and enduring transformation to a leadership culture of inclusion, empowerment, trust and teamwork. The Region showed markedly improved morale and reduced personnel turbulence. We attracted the best candidates as our organization expanded to support our business growth and market expansion.

ECQ #3: Results Driven

Tip: It is easy to use a Project Management slant for Results Driven, which can become a process-oriented story. However, the QRB is looking for a 60,000-foot view of a leader's ability to focus and lead an organization to produce results. Be sure to include plenty of actions and results from the executive level, avoiding a narrower focus; include quantifiable results to system improvements. Use opening and closing paragraphs that highlight why improving results was critical to the organization's mission.

Results Driven ECQ Example 1
Created a New Organizational Structure for Agency (Federal to SES)

▶ Before

Holding various positions within the federal government, I have a proven track record of getting results through people and sound management. For example, in my current piston as the Director of Workforce Planning and Management, Congress directed my Agency in Fiscal Year Conference Reports to "improve the management of FTE's, including forecasting, tracking, and monitoring the agency's FTEs. The committees also stressed disappointment with the agency's management of FTEs and suggested that continued mismanagement with no longer be tolerated. I recommended to the Agency that the FTE management program be transferred from the Budget Office to my office to ensure all inclusive Workforce Planning efforts. I also ensured him that I would fix the FTE management problem and improve our relationship with Congress. My request was granted and I won approval from the Appropriations committee to realign these functions to my office. Once the realignment was completed, I met with staffers from both the House and Senate (weekly) to gain a better understanding of their issues and concerns about our agency.

After analyzing the FTE issue and evaluating the current process, I discovered that the agency was hardly managing FTEs and was using an excel spreadsheet for tracking purposes. The agency was also severally underutilizing our FTES, had prematurely placed the agency on a hiring freeze, and was uncertain about how positions and FTEs were actually recorded. To correct the FTE management problem, I first reviewed the current and historical FTE reports, reviewed the spreadsheet maintained by the Budget Office, and evaluated the 10 appropriations and their associated FTE Caps and utilization. I then reviewed the current methodology for forecasting FTEs and concluded that the methodology was flawed and did not project end-of-year FTE utilization correctly. I immediately developed a new methodology for forecasting and monitoring FTEs.

What is wrong with the above essay? Check all that apply:

❏ The story lacks results

❏ Project management oriented, as opposed to leadership oriented

❏ Spelling and grammatical errors

▶ After

(Challenge) As the new Director, Workforce Planning and Management, I learned that employees were complaining that their grade levels were inconsistent across the Agency, leading to numerous Equal Employment Opportunity complaints.

(Context) As a result, several managers began meeting with me to discuss options for "reorganization" and methods to resolve the perceived problems with the grade levels. In addition, EEO had contacted me to discuss grade disparities across the Agency and asked for my advice on how best to address the "poor perception" and the concerns of employees and managers across the agency.

(Action) To address these challenges, I initiated an Agency-wide review of the organizational structure. During this review, I requested (and was approved) from the Agency head to put a moratorium on all organizational changes until the study was completed. I approved and recommended disposition for all Agency-wide position actions, organizational actions, and any issues relating to the organizational structure of the Agency. The study revealed that the Agency did not have a consistent organizational structure, supervisory ratios varied for like functions, grade levels were incorrectly classified, and inappropriate elevated divisions and inappropriate levels of management (the organizational structure) were driving the grade levels for positions (which appeared to be the root problem). I took a global review of how the Agency was structured, grouping organizational entities by work functions and mission. The analysis revealed that the Agency, as a requisite, needed a consistent structure and appropriate functional groupings.

(Action) Working with the Employee and Classification Branch under the Human Resources Division, I held high-level meetings with managers, supervisors, and senior level management to convey and diagram the inconsistencies and inherent problems with the organizational structure, the cause of their growing problems, and gain their buy-in for the newly proposed Agency-wide organizational structure (that would result in consistency across all organizations). This was a politically charged issue across the spectrum of employees; therefore I determined a plan of action to eliminate internal and external (our stakeholders—Congress) problems.

(Result) I designed a politically sensitive strategy and transformed the entire organizational structure resulting in a drastic reduction of EEO complaints (from 11 to one), the elevation of numerous positions to appropriate grade levels, and a future plan for reducing grade levels that were incorrectly classified. My strategy ensured that current employees were not monetarily affected by the decrease in grade levels, supervisory levels were not reduced until attrition occurred, and employees were briefed on the changes and were explained the "benefits" of the new structure (winning support—even if their grade was negatively impacted). I provided focus for a communication plan for stakeholders (Congress) explaining the new changes, remaining sensitive to negative or disparate assumptions. The organizational structure and full strategy that I proposed was approved by the Agency, the Senate and House Appropriations Committees, and the EEO and HR Divisions, and was implemented.

Results Driven ECQ Example 2

Created Profitable Operations (Industry to SES)

▶ After Only

(Challenge) When appointed General Manager, Consumer Goods USA at the Headquarters in Long Beach, California, I was challenged to turn around a business that had been hemorrhaging cash for the previous two years due to lackluster leadership and no strategic business focus. Despite the company's purchase of two plants with capacity to fulfill more than 20% of market demand, the domestic organization and business had not been properly developed. High-margin premium brands were handled by an exports division, depriving the local market of much-needed profits to fund investments to grow the organization and build the domestic business. In addition to these daunting business challenges, I assessed the plants' staff as lacking motivation, drive, and initiative. I essentially faced a "start-up" situation.

(Context) As a business leader and military officer, I routinely formulate and manage business and operational plans for the organizations I lead, including staffing plans for hundreds of personnel in many offices and plants across five countries and administration of operational and marketing budgets up to $20 million. I create highly profitable strategic plans for my company.

(Action) Within two months, I developed a strategy to address the personnel and business issues I faced. My immediate focus was improving the staff's attitude and professionalism to establish the right corporate culture as the organization expanded to develop the domestic market. In parallel, I aligned the organization behind key business processes focused on the development of the domestic market, which I established as the number one priority for the entire organization. I initiated a hiring and sales training program that produced a trained and ready domestic sales force that went from 10 to 70 employees in only four months. I streamlined and grew the distributor network from one to 10 in a six-month period, ensuring national distribution of our brands. I streamlined the locally produced brand portfolio, discontinuing low-volume brands, thereby achieving manufacturing efficiencies and focusing sales and marketing activities behind strategic priority mid-price brands.

(Result) These actions demonstrated to corporate leadership that I had set the conditions for a robust domestic sales and distribution organization. I easily achieved transfer to my control of the high-margin premium brands that were managed by the export division. I instituted sales and marketing programs to fully align and motivate the staff, the sales force, and the trade behind the newfound total brand portfolio concept. Within six months, the company doubled its sales volume with domestic sales. This achievement resulted in record-high sales volume. Just as important, the company showed a profit for the first time in three years. Additionally, I implemented other cost saving measures that brought an immediate savings of $5 million to the company; overall I created a very successful consumer goods market in the USA.

ECQ #4: Business Acumen

Tip: Use one or two stories that cover all three of the competencies for Business Acumen (Financial Management, Human Capital Management, and Technology Management). Your example should integrate all the aspects of business management. Recruitment is also important; OPM looks for creative management—for example, using detail assignments for temporary employees, or acting under tight deadlines.

Business Acumen ECQ Example 1
Secured Location for University-Hosted National Center for Forensic Science (Federal to SES)

▶ Before

I am a seasoned senior manager, with an established record of success in leveraging utilizing resources effectively. Resource management is critical to the success of any organization; creative resource management can make or break an organization in today's cost-conscious, streamlined environment. My success in managing resources was demonstrated when I led the planning required to secure a location for the University-hosted National Center for Forensic Science.

The University of Central Florida had been newly designated as host of the National Center for Forensic Science. Funding was available for the Center's computer forensics mission set, but not for separate and distinct office space or a facility. The University, in its proposal to host the Center, had noted anticipated synergistic benefits of co-locating this Center alongside other federal, state university, and private sector entities with expertise in simulation, modeling, and training that could be applied to computer forensics.

As a strong leader, I believed I could obtain a state-funded facility on federal land in exchange for office space for federal employees. I supervised a team to brainstorm ideas and determine if, and how, a joint-use facility could be constructed on located property. I built consensus and develop a proposal, which I presented to obtain the necessary approvals. My presentations to all stakeholders focused on the untapped opportunities to create synergy among public and private partners to position the state to be increasingly competitive in attracting federal funding. Under my leadership, the necessary approvals were approved. I also coordinated with appropriate staff and elected officials to obtain approval for state appropriations to cover construction costs.

My leadership resulted in the construction of a joint-use public-private facility dedicated to simulation and training, public safety, and forensic science.

> **What is wrong with the above essay? Check all that apply:**
>
> ❏ This essay is short
> ❏ It does not address the full CCAR format
> ❏ It includes a "belief"

▶ After

(Challenge) I spearheaded a challenge to lead the planning required to secure a location for the University-hosted National Center for Forensic Science; the University of Central Florida had been newly designated as host. Funding was available for the Center's computer forensics mission set, but not for separate and distinct office space or a facility. The University, in its proposal to host the Center, had noted anticipated synergistic benefits of co-locating this Center alongside other federal, state university, and private sector entities with expertise in simulation, modeling, and training that could be applied to computer forensics.

(Context) Finding a positive solution for the facility, including facility funding for a consolidated center of excellence, would be a challenge. Military partners noted constraints of no available office space and a 10-year horizon for new military construction (MILCON). University officials could not identify vacant property or office space. Private sector partners were not able to develop solutions acceptable to legal review.

(Action) To address this challenge, I envisioned a state-funded facility on federal land (no-cost lease) in exchange for office space for federal employees. I led a team to brainstorm ideas, work through barriers, and find solutions. To energize the team around a potential solution, I had identified 12 acres of vacant federal land nearby. I guided the team to determine if, and how, a joint-use facility could be constructed on this property. I led all efforts to develop a proposal to obtain the necessary approvals. My presentations to all stakeholders focused on untapped opportunities to create synergy among public and private partners to position the state to be increasingly competitive in attracting federal funding. Under my leadership, the necessary approvals from Congress, State of Florida, University, DOD, DOJ, Navy Facilities and Engineering Command, Research Park authorities, local regulatory bodies, and others were approved. Simultaneously, I coordinated with appropriate staff and elected officials to obtain approval for state appropriations to cover construction costs. Unanimous approvals were granted, principals signed binding agreements, and planning for the facility began.

(Result) My leadership, creativity, and tenacity resulted in the construction of a joint-use public-private facility dedicated to simulation and training, public safety, and forensic science. Tenants included the National Center for Forensic Science, Naval Air Warfare Center Training Systems Division offices, university research laboratories, offices, and training rooms available to local public safety professionals. I had the foresight to obtain advance authority to facilitate streamlined lease amendments for any future facilities construction. My collaborative efforts to champion teams to bring innovative concepts and ideas to reality has led to continuous partnering and growth among public and private partners with simulation and modeling expertise. Today, three Partnership Buildings populate the once vacant site due to my success in leveraging and utilizing resources effectively.

Business Acumen ECQ Example 2

NSPS (Federal to SES)

▶ After Only

(Challenge) Our organization was part of the first wave to transition from the General Schedule (GS) to the National Security Personnel System (NSPS) performance-based system in the Department of the Army, so leading this effort was unique and challenging. Since this type of work had never been done in our organization, I led with a flexible attitude to meet our hard deadline and to have all the performance plans and tools in place to implement the NSPS performance-based system.

(Context) My team met with other federal audit agencies that had performance-based rating systems to obtain ideas and lessons learned to provide guidance in developing these new tools, business rules, and policies to implement NSPS.

(Action) I designed and implemented human capital strategies to meet organizational mission and goals. I led and focused a five-person Process Action Team (PAT) established to develop performance and developmental expectations, policy, and procedures to fully implement the National Security Personnel System (NSPS) for the Army Audit Service.

(Action) Through my leadership on the Process Action Team, I guided my team in full development of the framework of human capital strategies to ensure Army Audit Service achieved these NSPS goals. For example, my vision included the creation of standardized performance plans for all three pay band levels, for each career field, for 1,200+ auditors and support personnel, aligned with the Army Audit Service mission and strategic goals. Army Audit Service Senior Leadership approved the use of the performance plans and Task Assignment Agreement forms to fully implement NSPS at Army Audit Service. My Process Action Team developed this automated system designed as a program management tool.

(Result) I successfully guided my team in meeting the due date, and management approved the performance plans, procedures, business rules, and tools. I achieved our strategic objective of implementing an effective and efficient NSPS performance-based plan. All 1,200 auditors attended all NSPS training, and 100 percent of supervisors performed and documented required employee feedback sessions. In addition, I was able to terminate seven poor performers, through use of this new tool, obtaining full endorsement from the Human Resources Officer and the assigned attorney.

In my NSPS performance rating, which received the highest rating of "5," my supervisor wrote, "Because of his exceptional leadership skills in developing solutions to respond to new issues, he was handpicked to lead the Army Audit Service process action team that developed the performance plans and tools to successfully implement NSPS."

ECQ #5: Building Coalitions

Tip: Building Coalitions reaches far beyond coordinating events and delivering speeches. Rather, it is about the need to create strong, focused coalitions with internal and external entities to promote the sharing of information and creation of harmony across boundaries. Make certain that the reader understands that you are working out program issues at senior levels in the organization. Also, demonstrate your ability to nurture lasting, long-term relationships.

Building Coalitions ECQ Example 1
Missile Defense Coalitions (Military to SES)

▶ Before

I believe this is my strongest area. It is most definitely the area I enjoy most, provided leading and working with people is integral. Team building, partnering and communications, both verbal and written, are extremely important to effective organizations. I have spent over 30 years in the military working in and improving on all these very skills. I have extensive experience leading and developing working relationships within organizations on up to interagency levels. I have worked with Congress and on Congressional actions, building personal political savvy that takes years to develop. I also have vast experience nurturing relationships, developing and enhancing alliances and engineering coalitions across a wide range of interests and cross-functional activities that includes extensive international work with our friends, allies and business partners.

During my time on the USEUCOM staff, I not only honed my U.S. political savvy during this period, I grew experience in international political savvy as well. Much of the experience I have related above and the evaluation quotes previously provided directly attribute to my coalition building and effective communication skills. However, to add some more specifics I will provide more evaluation comments:

"Difficult period in a difficult command dispersed over three geographic areas yet still able to coalesce his team to provide ever increasing support at all levels, including NATO and Joint Service Commands, significantly improving support and quality of life for all."

"My Number One of 44 Officers of all designators including two more senior."

"The finest Naval Officer it has been my pleasure to command. The Number

One officer of 45 assigned, including four more senior. Recognized bedrock of the community. Equally adept at handling the concerns of Flag Officers and E-1's alike."

"Keynote speaker… Commencement speaker… Community spokesman…

Always out front at every community event. Superb written and oral communicator."

"Highly lauded team builder who inspires cooperation. Promoted a positive working climate within a diverse group of people across all directorates in his host command. Built a superb team of missile defense experts who will represent warfighter interests for years to come. Recognized throughout USSTRATCOM as the MDA expert. His efforts as the single point of contact at the MDA representing USSTRATCOM and the entire mission area of Global Ballistic Missile Defense (GBMD) has been near heroic. He has developed dozens of personal and hundreds of professional relationships through innovative methods that have notably enhanced unit cohesion and directly improved command climate between two very large organizations. His ad hoc team leadership and sheer breadth of situational awareness regarding missile defense actions means his expertise and honest broker opinion is sought after by all. His unprecedented personal initiative, combined with his mature seasoned Pentagon and political savvy, have been critical toward accomplishing the President of the United States National Security Directive to accelerate and "operationalize" GBMD."

"A gifted leader...superb handling of Joint Staff and Congressional staffs...outstanding reputation throughout EUCOM, Theater Component Commands, NATO/SHAPE staffs, Joint Chiefs/OSD Staff Officers and Congressional Staff Members." "A charismatic leader... superb leadership of his 50-member Congressional Issues Team through the fast-reaction, high pressure testimony cycle...outstanding leadership with CINC/DCINC/Component Commander/ NATO and U.S. staffs during more than 90 CODEL visits comprising 354 Members of Congress [during a one-year period]...Community Leader and Core Values Ambassador." "Key community leader. Elected as the J-5 Directorate CMEO [Command Equal Opportunity Officer]. Absolute role model of fairness and respect. Recognized pro-active community EO leader."

What is wrong with the above essay? Check all that apply:

❏ The original essay is jumbled with quotes from performance evaluations

❏ Filled with acronyms

❏ Unfocused

❏ Not in the CCAR format

❏ Too long

Remember, don't write opinions about yourself, and don't quote evaluations in your ECQ narratives.

▶ After

(Challenge) I was working at the Missile Defense Agency (MDA) as the sole military representative for U.S. Strategic Command when the President issued a National Security Presidential Directive ordering the DOD to take all measures necessary to field an initial Missile Defense capability within two years.

(Context) U.S. Strategic Command (USSTRATCOM) served as the military advocate for DOD.

(Action) Using transformational policy that I wrote, USSTRATCOM was given the mission of "Global" [strategic directly linked to theater] Missile Defense and authority as the primary military interlocutor to the MDA. As such, I guided the design, building, and implementation of a coalition between USSTRATCOM, the Pentagon staff (including the Military Services) and the regional Combatant Commands; establishing formal policy, processes, and procedures for conducting military Missile Defense operations. I also built a lasting coalition for continued research, development, and acquisition for Warfighter Involvement Process.

(Result) Prior to the deadline, under Presidential authority, the Secretary of Defense declared Initial Defensive Operations for the Ballistic Missile Defense System (BMDS). I was awarded a Joint Service Achievement Medal for my actions leading to this declaration and a Defense Meritorious Service Medal for my achievements while serving as the USSTRATCOM Representative to the MDA.

(Sub-story) I also built a solid coalition between the National Reconnaissance Office (NRO) and the MDA, which is expanding to other Intelligence Community (IC) organizations. For more than five years, there has been a direct relationship between the MDA and the NRO; however, no documents codifying this relationship existed when I began working at the NRO. I drafted and staffed an overarching Memorandum of Agreement (MOA), which was ultimately signed by the Director NRO and Director MDA. That MOA serves as the keystone document for myriad engagements and formal [funded] projects between these two organizations. Subsequently I authored, at the NRO's request, the MDA Engagement Plan. These engagement plans act as the NRO's primary strategic communication outlining and directing activities between major coalition partners. I briefed my MDA Engagement Plan to an approving board, which accepted the plan with minor changes. My plan was ultimately approved and placed into final staffing process for NRO Director signature.

Building Coalitions ECQ Example 2

Audit Coalition (Federal to SES)

▶ After Only

(Challenge) As the Audit Director, I led an audit to coordinate and develop relationships with Senior Leadership officials from 12 different Department of Defense (DOD) and Department of Army Commands and Activities worldwide. This audit was conducted in Djibouti, Africa (acquisition audit) and in Bahrain (disbursing audit). This was particularly difficult, as we were only allotted 150 days to complete the audit work on-site, 49 percent less time than is standard to complete this type of audit.

(Context) No operating agreement existed between the Command and Activities, which created a "turf battle" over who had ultimate accountability and responsibility for the key contracting and disbursing functional areas. This led to confusion amongst the Commands in terms of who would perform the corrective actions relating to audit findings and recommendations. As such, I remained sensitive to the political landscape in leading this multi-location audit.

(Action) I initiated communication with senior military (Joint) managers for each of the key functional areas to address roles and responsibilities to eliminate confusion and duplication of services. I networked with colleagues from their parent Commands to identify solutions and gather information on "best practices" for managing similar joint operations with multiple commands and activities. I shared this information with the senior military managers and recommended the establishment of a working group to clarify roles and responsibilities; to determine the best contracting and disbursing organizational structure to support their strategic mission; and to respond to our recommendations. There were serious conflicts among the groups as to what the report should address and the direction of recommendations. As the overseer, I often mediated the disputes. I briefed six Flag Officers from the major commands to gain their support, and obtained their full endorsement before the report was issued.

(Action) The working group/coalition was established with the 12 DOD command and activities, and from this working group's recommendations, the Department of Defense established my organization as the Executive Agent for providing contracting and disbursing support to the sites. This eliminated the confusion as to who should respond to the audit findings and recommendations, and the "turf battles" between the commands. Due to my leadership, 19 recommendations were presented to the consortium that included: change business practices and processes and reduce disbursing and contracting operation risks; improve the efficiency and effectiveness of disbursing and contracting operations; and strengthen the integrity and adequacy of these checks and balances to prevent fraud, waste, and abuse.

(Result) All 12 DOD disbursing and contracting Command Activities concurred with the recommendations and took immediate action to improve the operations. All six Flag Officers fully endorsed the audit, praised the report results, and recommended to the Auditor General of the Army the establishment of an audit office in Naples, Italy to provide audit coverage for the entire Europe, Africa, and Asia region.

Technical Qualifications

Technical Qualifications (TQs) are executive level "knowledge, skills, and abilities" (KSAs) required by agencies and identified on job announcements. They may also be called the Mandatory Technical Qualifications (MTQs), Mandatory Technical Competencies (MTCs), or Professional Technical Qualifications (PTQs). TQs are specific to the position and agency, and may be written as separate one- or two-page essays addressing each TQ for a traditional executive federal resume and ECQ application package, or integrated into a five-page resume-based application (per the job announcement). Candidates will be required to demonstrate experience and skills sufficient to successfully perform the duties and responsibilities of a particular executive level position by describing superior technical qualifications and technical knowledge.

Many executive positions have specific subject-matter knowledge and skill/competency requirements that candidates must meet. The TQs are competencies that agencies may identify specific to the position being filled. Well-written TQs indicate a required level of proficiency in a functional area. The examples/accomplishments/stories used for TQs need to express executive level proficiency.

Major Difference Between TQs and ECQs

TQs involve specific executive subject-matter expertise, knowledge, and/or technical leadership.

ECQs are executive leadership qualities that are transferable to any agency in government.

The TQs are drafted in the CCAR format, like ECQs, for the traditional essay package; they can be reframed and used as short summary paragraphs, integrated into the five-page resume-based application. TQs describe functional areas of expertise, and can be used as screen-out factors for HR specialists and hiring managers. Hiring managers are seeking highly qualified candidates who have current knowledge of a specific subject matter. So use recent stories (within the past ten years), describe expertise directly related to the TQs, and use the language/keywords from the TQs and the duty description section of the job announcement within the TQ narratives. Avoid using laundry lists.

Rewrite your ECQ stories from a different angle to fit a TQ. Some candidates believe that the TQs are less important and they spend less time developing the TQ responses; however, the hiring agency is very interested in a candidate's TQs to help score knowledge, skills, and abilities. TQs can be similar stories to ECQs, if a TQ is the same or has nearly the same requirements as an ECQ. For example, if a TQ reads: "Describe any experience you have supervising and/or managing personnel in the accomplishment of major projects, please include the nature and scope of the work supervised," you may be able to draw from a story you developed for Leading People and rewrite the story with a different point of view—focusing on the agency's needs and other specific requirements gleaned from the vacancy announcement.

TQs may need to be rewritten for varied job announcements, as the qualifications may not be the same for each announcement; whereas ECQs often can remain static, because they are focused on specific leadership competencies. TQ bullets may also need to be replaced on a five-page resume-based application, tailoring the resume to the specific TQs from a different announcement.

Technical Qualification Samples

Example #1:

Describe experience in formulating, developing, implementing, and revising policies, strategies, and processes for national security programs related to natural or other disasters and emergency response.

(Challenge) A post-Katrina evaluation of FEMA's hurricane response caused changes to be made to align all federal agencies to one National Incident Management System (NIMS). The Air Force Incident Management System (AFIMS) was created to mirror NIMS as the AF emergency response structure. I was challenged to align the old response organization, its people, processes, and structure to the new system. This involved reorganizing how medical, safety, law enforcement, fire, caregiver, and command and control responded to emergencies, were allocated and managed, to best target and maximize the response. My vision was to revamp the process and build an organization with a broader focus that could handle multiple emergencies effectively.

(Context) Supporting a large Air Force base (AFB), I led a 1,700-person organization operating the base infrastructure. Additionally, I was the On-Scene Director for the Disaster Control Group, leading responses to real-world and simulated emergencies in a 14-state region.

(Action) I began building relationships beyond the installation to provide broader community support. I visited state Emergency Management Agencies (EMA) meeting with directors and detailing my plans for a collaborative effort. I also visited the local Army National Guard to establish mutual support agreements for transportation, airlift, explosive ordnance and biological/chemical support. I dispatched medical experts to local hospitals to establish emergency support agreements. I revised on-scene command and control. To prepare these mid-level leaders to lead during a wide range of emergencies, and to communicate effectively with the higher-level Emergency Operations Center (EOC), I worked with emergency response stakeholders to create realistic, multi-scenario training simulations. During repeated exercises, first responder leadership and communication skills dramatically improved.

As the EOC Director, I created an installation EOC to provide command and control, funded the construction necessary for the EOC to operate, and directed the renovation of the communication suite to ensure contact with first responders in the field. The EOC managed all aspects of an emergency including first responder oversight; state and local liaison; media inquiries; higher level reporting requirements; and reported directly to senior installation leadership. I also created space within the EOC for state and local agencies to operate.

(Result) I guided the transformation of the organization's emergency response apparatus from a traditional, locally focused disaster control element, to a nationally oriented emergency management machine, merging Air Force, state and local emergency response agencies into one powerful emergency management operation, capable of managing multiple events, while effectively coordinating response actions, with many internal and external stakeholders. I established an AFIMS-compliant EOC in just eight months, 33% ahead of schedule. My actions elevated the AFB to national level compliance and provided a broader, more effective capability for the Air Force. For actual and follow-on simulated emergency situations, I reduced the response time needed to establish multi-event command and control by approximately 15-30 minutes—a significant improvement in this critical, life-and-death, time-sensitive environment.

Example #2:
Experience in developing and implementing organization-wide operations and processes for deployment, security, and oversight of large scale technology services, and leading broad cultural change in information technology management roles.

(Challenge) I faced the challenge of persuading numerous Agency law enforcement components to support the Law Enforcement Information Sharing Program by publishing shareable law enforcement information that could be accessed by other federal, state, local, and tribal law enforcement agencies via databases.

(Context) As Deputy Director for e-Gov and Information Sharing in the Office of the Chief Information Officer, I was hired to execute the program. The Law Enforcement Information Sharing Program (LEISP) is the Agency's program to share law enforcement information routinely across jurisdictional boundaries to prevent terrorism, and to systematically improve the investigation and prosecution of criminal activity. The LEISP is a program focused on changing the culture of law enforcement information sharing from "need to know" to "need to share."

(Action) I began by working with colleagues and contractors to focus the reallocation of resources so a data distribution facility could be designed, developed, and deployed within existing budget thresholds. The LEISP data distribution facility was designed to support the publishing and distribution of more than 100 million records. Once built, the facility allowed the Department's law enforcement components to publish shareable law enforcement information to be shared with one or more technology-based information sharing systems.

Second, my senior colleagues and I established a governance framework to monitor the execution of the Law Enforcement Information Sharing Program strategy and compliance with policies promulgated by the Deputy Attorney General. I co-led the LEISP Coordinating Committee (LCC) with the Deputy Attorney General, and provided oversight of the large law enforcement information effort. During meetings, I briefed the LCC metrics on the law enforcement components compliance, describing law enforcement information to be shared in the system.

Third, I guided development of a process to engage state and local law enforcement agencies to create law enforcement information sharing partnerships, including getting local U.S. Attorney and Agency law enforcement field office support. The process I designed also included steps to ensure state and local law enforcement agencies could adhere to prescribed security guidelines and requirements for vetting users who would view the Agency's law enforcement information.

(Result) My work to execute LEISP led directly to a dramatic expansion of shareable law enforcement data from 22 million records to more than 60 million records, and an increase in state and local partnerships from six to more than 32. My leadership of this process enabled well over 2,900 federal, state, local, and tribal law enforcement agencies to enter into productive nationwide information sharing partnerships across the broader federal law enforcement and intelligence community.

Example #3:

Experience in developing and implementing organization-wide operations and processes for advanced engineering and manufacturing operations and addressing specific needs or challenges.

(Challenge) When I joined the corporation, the company had not met or passed Sarbanes-Oxley compliance in two years, it did not have any policies in place for guidance within the ERP system, and many different functional areas were overlapping into other functional areas of responsibility. The lack of procedural guidance caused great confusion; manufacturing had control of costing and labor routings and standards; purchasing was able to change suppliers without following Engineering Procedures for approval; any staff had access to engineering Bill of Materials and could change parts, routings, and material requirements at will; and purchasing had capability to change raw material or component cost without approval or costing by accounting.

(Context) As Corporate Vice President of Engineering, I led an Enterprise Resource Planning (ERP) upgrade to meet Sarbanes-Oxley compliance for the corporation (with 27 plants across the nation, and plants in Mexico and Japan), with annual revenue more than $1.2 billion. I was recruited to assume the additional responsibility to bring three separate operational structures into one, joining the corporation under one Product Engineering (R&D) Division.

(Action) I formed a senior working group including the Director of Information Systems, Director of Accounting, Director of Manufacturing, and Director of Customer Service to develop and write policies to ensure compliance with Sarbanes-Oxley and create an entire "chain of command" and flow chart to ensure departments managed their own assigned functional responsibilities. The newly documented policies and procedures prevented duplication and lost items, and ensured streamlined processes and a standardized process for each department across the corporation, plus it eliminated any functional area or person having access that would create a conflict of interest. I focused the working group's writing of the new policies, which I presented before the Executive Management Council and Board of Directors for unanimous approval. I then introduced my vision and strategy for rollout of the new policies.

(Challenge & Action) Overseeing this transformation was a challenge. I encountered strong resistance in some functional areas, and I worked with senior managers to solve pushbacks and defuse animosities. Due to the reestablishment of authority levels, all departments corporate-wide were involved in the changes to ensure compliance with Sarbanes-Oxley. Under my direction, the leadership staff developed and implemented a comprehensive training program for corporate-wide implementation including webinars and presentations/awareness meetings to smooth emotions and gain consensuses across the corporation, at all levels, and within all the functional departments. I personally traveled to all sites to meet with leadership.

(Result) Guiding a team of senior managers at all sites, all departments adopted and implemented the new processes. During an inspection, only three months after implementation, the entire company met inspection requirements—the first time ever that the corporation met and exceeded the Sarbanes-Oxley requirements. The transformation was so successful, my program was requested as a model process for other interested corporations, and I was the invited guest speaker at the Association of Executive Manufacturers.

Chapter Five

Three SES Application Formats

Federal agencies now have a choice of using one of three processes for filling SES positions: the traditional format, the resume-based format, and the accomplishment record.

Each federal agency determines which application process to use, and each federal vacancy announcement posted for SES positions or SES CDP will specifically indicate which format is required by that agency for the posted position. Not only are there three different general formats available for agencies to choose from, agencies are not required to follow the standard OPM template for each of these formats and will often modify them or even create hybrid methods. Therefore, it is critical to read each vacancy announcement thoroughly before applying for positions. Applicants may now be required to create two or three types of SES application packages with the associated required documents to apply for a variety of agencies.

Obviously, this diversity of application methods translates into a challenge for the applicant.

In this book we will only address how to write the traditional and resume-based formats, but with the techniques and tips we provide, you will be prepared to address any of the application formats or requirements that you may encounter.

Our recommendation is to prepare the longest application format first—the traditional format—and be prepared to edit it down for the other variations.

Three Most Common SES Application Formats

Traditional

The traditional SES application format is the lengthiest of the three described here—easily reaching 20 pages for a complete application package.

- Executive Federal Resume—three to five pages (including all the required federal elements, i.e., vacancy number, name, address, phone, email, job titles, dates, hours worked, salary, duties, accomplishments, education with dates, additional information)
- TQs—one or two pages, based on the vacancy announcement instructions
- ECQs—two examples or stories for each ECQ in the CCAR format, up to 8,000 characters each or 10 pages maximum, drawing from recent experience during the past 10 years
    o Leading Change
    o Leading People
    o Results Driven
    o Business Acumen
    o Building Coalitions
- Cover Letter

Resume-Based

This format and the next, the accomplishment record, were designed to be more streamlined and less burdensome than the traditional SES application format. The resume-based option was designed especially for high-level executive positions with difficult-to-meet requirements that would limit the number of applicants.

- Five-Page SES Federal Resume (with ECQs and TQs integrated within the context of the resume)
- Cover Letter

Accomplishment Record

This method requires applicants to submit a resume and a shorter set of narratives addressing specific competencies (usually one from each ECQ). The essays are usually limited to one page each. See also an SES CDP announcement with an Accomplishment Record requirement on pages 142-145.

- Executive Federal Resume
- Selected Competencies—review announcement for page length
- Cover Letter

Sample Announcements: Traditional Format

The best way to identify whether a vacancy announcement is requesting the traditional format application is the length of the ECQ essays, which will be specified to be ten pages. See the highlighted page lengths below.

Example: Environmental Protection Agency

> How To Apply
> Your narrative responses to the Executive Core Qualification statements (ECQs) should not exceed two pages per each ECQ and not more than 10 pages total. Your narrative responses to the Mandatory Technical and/or Desirable factors should not exceed two pages per each factor.
>
> You must provide specific examples of your education, experience, training and awards in the manner and order instructed below which are applicable to each: (A) Executive Core Qualifications (ECQs), (B) Technical Qualifications (TQs), and (C) Desirable Qualifications (DQs). Response to the five ECQs and TQs is mandatory. Failure to address the ECQs and TQs will result in your application being disqualified. Addressing the DQs is optional; however, not addressing them will impact your rating.

Example: U.S. Department of Agriculture

> **MANDATORY QUALIFICATIONS**
> (Fully describe your qualifications for each Executive Core Qualification and Technical Qualification statements as an attachment with your application package).
>
> Applicants are encouraged to contact xxxx at 301-504-0000, SeniorPositions@ars.usda.gov to obtain information on preparing your application package for this position in the Senior Executive Service.
>
> **HOW TO APPLY:**
> You must submit your application so that it will be received by the closing date of the announcement.
>
> 1. OF-612, Application for Federal Employment, OR resume that includes all specific information that your application must contain except your social security number (see 'Applying for a Federal Job: and forms at www.opm.gov./forms/html/of.asp)
>
> 2. Complete responses to executive and technical qualifications. (Managerial statements, i.e., ECQ's must not exceed 10 pages). Visit www.opm.gov./ses/recruitment/qualify.asp for additional guidance on writing your Qualifications Statements.

Sample Announcements: Five-Page SES Federal Resume Format

Example: Federal Aviation Administration

HOW TO APPLY:

Submit a current resume which describes your qualifications. Your resume must not exceed five pages including an optional cover letter. Information beyond five pages will not be evaluated.

Applications may be submitted electronically via email to xxxx@dot.gov or via fax at (202) 366-0000 and must be received by 11:59 pm Eastern Standard Time on the announcement closing date. If you have questions, call xxxx at (202) 366-0000 or xxxx at (202) 366-0000.

Example: Veterans Administration

REQUIRED DOCUMENTS:

A complete application for this position includes the following items:

1. Resume which demonstrates your experience, accomplishment, training, education and awards reflecting your ability to meet each of the MANDATORY executive core qualification requirement(s) for this position. Elaborate on your experience and accomplishments, highlighting your level of responsibilities, scope and complexity of programs managed, work objectives met (the results of your efforts), policy initiatives and level of contacts. Ensure your resume does not exceed five (5) pages. Information beyond the five page resume will not be evaluated. DO NOT submit the application form OF-612, Optional Application for Federal Employment in lieu of a resume. DO NOT submit separate narrative responses to address the executive core qualifications.

2. Complete responses to the Online Questionnaire. View Occupational Questionnaire

HOW TO APPLY:

We strongly encourage you to apply online. To begin, click the Apply Online button and follow the prompts to register and submit all required documents. To return to your saved application, login in to your USAJOBS account at http://www.usajobs.opm.gov/ and click on "Application Status". Click on the position title, and then select Apply Online to continue.

> If you are unsure about the application instructions, call or write the point of contact listed in the announcement.
>
> Don't wait until the last minute to write and ask questions about the application. Think ahead and give yourself plenty of time.

Sample Announcements: SES Career Development Program (CDP)

Job Title: Senior Executive Service Candidate Development Program
SALARY RANGE: $116,021.00 to $158,700.00 / Per Year
SERIES & GRADE: GS-0301-15
POSITION INFORMATION: Part-Time - Developmental Program 12-24 months – Permanent
PROMOTION POTENTIAL: 15

The Senior Executive Service Candidate Development Program (SES CDP) offers the opportunity for exceptionally talented and well qualified individuals to receive structured professional development and to gain valuable executive experience. Participants in the program engage in developmental assignments and formal training activities to enhance their executive competencies and to increase their awareness of public policy, programs, and issues. A 360 degree assessment will be administered to determine areas which need to be developed or strengthened during the program. All CDP participants must be available for assignments and training in the Washington, D.C. area and and other areas that may be identified throughout the United States. Upon successful completion of the program, you will be eligible to request certification of your executive qualifications from the Office of Personnel Management (OPM). Certified candidates may be placed non-competitively into senior executive service positions for which they are qualified. Successful program participation, in all segments, is required; however, it does not guarantee certification or placement in an SES position.

EXECUTIVE CORE QUALIFICATION NARRATIVES ARE LIMITED TO ONE (1) PAGE PER ECQ AND CAN NOT EXCEED 5 PAGES TOTAL.

This is a 12-24 month, part-time developmental program. Participants will continue to occupy their regular positions except while they are attending formal training, seminars, discussions, conferences, or while on rotational assignments. The minimum SES CDP components include:

- Orientation (one week)
- Two 360-degree Assessments (pre & post) & workshop debrief
- 80-hour Interagency Leadership Training
- Rotational Assignment(s)
- ECQ Enrichment (leadership training & site visits)
- Continual Learning Seminars (seminars and workshops)
- Peer Learning Circles (monthly, one-hour, facilitated calls for candidates to share ideas)
- Executive Coaching (four, one-hour sessions covering various topics)
- Coaching on Final ECQ Writing

QUALIFICATIONS REQUIRED:
To be minimally qualified, the SES Candidate Development Program requires that individuals have at least one year of experience that is equivalent to the GS-15 level. Candidates must then demonstrate competence or potential for development in the five SES Executive Core Qualifications (ECQs) which are the leadership criteria defined by the Office of Personnel Management (OPM) to certify candidates for SES positions. OPM will certify candidates primarily on their demonstrated mastery of the ECQs.

When addressing the ECQs, applicants should include one notable example using the Challenge-Context-Action-Result (CCAR) model. All applicants must answer the online questions, submit a resume and a five-page ECQ narrative (one example per ECQ in CCAR format; do not exceed five pages). All applicants must address each ECQ separately and are required to respond to all ECQs. If you fail to do so, you will be rated as "ineligible."

HOW YOU WILL BE EVALUATED:
Phase I: Initial Review of Application Package
Phase II: Executive Resources Board Evaluation
Phase III: Interviews
Phase IV: Senior Executive Evaluation
Phase V: Selection

See another sample SES CDP announcement on pages 142-145.

Agency-Specific Requirements

Many agencies hire senior executive level and senior professional or SES-equivalent candidates using application requirements specific to the agency. SES candidates' ECQs are certified by a Qualifications Review Board, according to OPM's requirements. Some excepted agencies and non-career SES positions may have different application requirements, which do not require approval through OPM or a QRB.

The bottom line is, if you prepare a full traditional version of an SES package with an executive federal resume, a full set of ECQ essays, and several TQ essays, you will be very prepared to draw from this portfolio of documents to respond to vacancy announcements from different agencies that post varied applications requirements, as the executive or senior level requirements and competencies for those requirements are often similar to ECQs. The more accomplishment stories you develop, the larger your library of stories to draw from in order to complete varied application packages. Moreover, the added benefit of preparing a full executive resume and ECQ package is that you will also be drafting content for the structured/behavior-based interview.

To help you prepare for varied announcement requirements, here is a short list of some of the different requirements you may encounter from various agencies when applying for SES, senior level, GS-15, or SES-equivalent positions. These requirements may be in addition to a resume, ECQs, cover letter, or other requirements. Application requirements may also vary within the same agency, so always be sure to review the application requirements thoroughly before applying for a position.

The **Federal Aviation Administration (FAA)** requests its executive applicants to complete Dimensions: 1. Achieving Operational Results; 2. Leading People; 3. Building Relationships; 4. Leading Strategic Change. These are separate essays in addition to the resume.

The **Intelligence Community (IC)** requires Senior Executive Officers to submit a Senior Officer Core Qualification (SOCQ) Standard—Leading the Intelligence Enterprise. This SOCQ Standard involves the ability to integrate resources, information, interests, and activities in support of the IC's mission and to lead and leverage cross-organizational collaborative networks. There are three competencies that need to be addressed on one page each: 1. Collaboration and Integration; 2. Enterprise Focus; and 3. Values-Centered Leadership.

Job announcements from the **Securities and Exchange Commission** requires a resume that integrates the specific knowledge, skills, and abilities, as well as competencies from a set of self-assessment questions. The resume may be written similar to the five-page resume-based application for SES.

The **Department of Defense** requests DOD-specific competencies to be addressed by SES applicants (during a phased approach) demonstrating that they possess the background, ability, and skill to lead across organizational and functional boundaries focusing on the three unique DOD competencies: 1. Enterprise Perspective; 2. Joint Perspective; and 3. National Security.

The **Department of the Air Force**'s SES application includes a four-page resume in a specified format, and a total of 21 pages for the resume, ECQs, and TQs.

Chapter Six

The Traditional SES Application

Components of the Traditional SES Application

The traditional application can be upward of 20 to 25 pages and may include:

- Executive federal resume
- Executive Core Qualifications (ECQs)
- Technical Qualifications (TQs)
- Executive cover letter (may be optional)
- Additional requirements as indicated, such as Desirable Qualifications or specific documentation, i.e. letter of interest, transcripts for licensure, etc.

This chapter also includes our first case study (Judy Johnson) with these components:

- Background information
- Before resume
- Top Ten List of Accomplishments
- After resume, paper format
- After resume, USAJOBS format
- Selected ECQs
- Cover letter

The Executive Federal Resume

The executive federal resume is used for applying to GS-15 and SES announcements and is prepared in the federal resume format. It may be submitted via a formatted (hard copy) document or an online resume builder. This resume is on average three to five pages and must include relevant Work Experience (from the last ten years), Education, Certifications, Awards, Training, and accomplishments that demonstrate your leadership skills.

The ECQ and TQ essays do not need to be included in the traditional format executive federal resume. However, the short accomplishments identified in the executive federal resume should be stories used in the ECQ essays. The HR professionals will verify and cross-reference that the stories you use in your ECQ essays are identified on your resume.

Executive federal resumes include more detailed descriptions of work experience, highlighting the scope and breadth of your leadership and focusing on the most recent ten years and summarizing positions held prior to ten years ago. This resume usually includes a short executive profile highlighting your most notable career achievements including the largest number of personnel you supervised, the largest budget you administered, your interactions with very senior level people, your overall ability to influence positive organizational performance on a far-reaching scale, and perhaps the addition of a notable award.

The resume should be drafted in reverse chronological order. It may include a brief description of each organization's operational scope (the size of the organization and its mission), combined with a short description of your leadership (duties), and a short list of bulleted accomplishments (key leadership initiatives) with results for each position. Accomplishments demonstrate your past performance and your knowledge, skills, and abilities needed for the position. When the organization's mission is noted, it is easier for you to describe within the context of your accomplishments how you led programs to meet the organizational mission and goals.

A careful analysis of an announcement and the major duties will reveal keywords and competencies that the HR professionals are seeking to qualify a candidate for a position. As you review an announcement, highlight keywords and themes within the position description and TQs, and integrate those words and themes into the achievements listed on your resume.

For example, if a duty description from a vacancy announcement is focused on leading a large staff and managing large budgets, then your resume will need to reflect your ability to lead large staffs and focus on fiscal management. If the announcement is focused on interacting with Congress and other senior level stakeholders in government and developing policy, then you will want to include examples that demonstrate your work with Congress and the development of policy for your organization, company, or agency. Use the major duties and TQs from a job announcement as a guide for developing the content of your resume.

Here is an example of identifying keywords and skills from an announcement for a Financial Services Director:

The incumbent exercises **executive leadership** in the following areas: **Principal advisor** who provides **authoritative advice** to the Director for **Fiscal Operations** and **Policy** and other officials, with policy and **operational advice** and **counsel** dealing with **financial, strategic initiatives and operations issues** affecting **Domestic Finance** and other Departmental **policy offices**.

Relationship Management. Provides direction and **guidance** to **financial agents** to **deliver identified services** and quickly **respond to changing circumstances**.

Provides **Management oversight** for the **financial agents** designated to provide services for programs throughout the Departmental Offices.

Directs a subordinate staff in **managing relationships** with financial agents on a daily basis, serving as a **central point of contact** for both the financial agents and the agency program offices that rely on the financial agents' services. The incumbent also **manages staff effectively** to enhance each individual's **professional development**.

Develops and issues policies to financial agents to **execute and support large, complex financial transactions**.

Provides **advice** on the broad **range of Federal fiscal operational** and policy issues.

Provides **advice and guidance** to **improve use of automation**.

The keywords and skills that are required and sometimes repeated in this announcement are bolded above. These are the words a candidate who is applying for this position would integrate into the resume.

Here is an example of how the keywords and skills may be integrated into content for a resume focused on the applicant's specific leadership scope:

As the Deputy, **Financial Operations**, I lead a **subordinate staff of six direct-report supervisors managing relationships** for a multi-functional team of 28 including **financial agents**, analysts, and administrative staff supporting 2,000 customers in 10 different offices spread across the nation.

Policy advisor to senior leadership for **fiscal operations** and **policy** development, responsible for presenting to the Agency Head and Congressional Budget Office a $4B adjustment to agency expenses in FY12.

Do:

- Use 12-point Times New Roman font and one-inch margins
- Include the announcement number on the resume
- Use recent, notable achievements, and quantify and qualify results
- List recent education, advanced training, or new credentials to enhance your qualifications
- Spell out acronyms in the first instance
- Use a combination of short paragraphs and bullets
- Ensure the resume expresses overall executive leadership experience
- Carefully analyze the announcements for major duties, keywords, TQs, and competencies required for the position
- Tailor each resume submission to meet the needs of the new vacancy announcement

Don't:

- Use too many bullets
- Use the big block style of writing (large blocks of text without breaks or bullets)
- Mix fonts or use fonts that are too small to read
- Describe personal beliefs or philosophies

Avoid these words:

- Assist with
- Helped with
- Other duties include
- Responsible for
- Participated in
- Duties include
- Personal beliefs or philosophies

These passive voice phrases and verbs are typically used in GS-5 to 11 federal resumes.

Instead, use active voice verbs to show your expertise and leadership.

Difference Between Paper and USAJOBS Format Resumes

The paper formatted resume is uploaded into USAJOBS and can include the following resume sections:

- Profile or Executive Summary at the top of the resume
- Areas of Expertise at the top of the resume
- Education and critical Certifications can be listed before Work Experience
- Work Experience – limit this section to 20 years
- Focus on the last ten years
- Other information, such as associations, boards, important memberships, pro bono work, publications, public speaking,

The USAJOBS resume is a format that will be copied and pasted into the USAJOBS Resume Builder. The resume builder format is sometimes required by the agency. For instance, NASA STARS system requires the USAJOBS builder. This resume organization is structured based on the builder fields:

- Name, address, personal info
- Work Experience
- Education
- Certifications and Training
- Memberships
- Additional Information

Case Study 1 – Military Officer/International Corporate Executive

Target Agency and Position: Executive Director, Mobilization & Training, Department Of Navy

Judy Johnson (name fictionalized) had an exciting and interesting parallel industry and military Reserve career for more than 20 years. She was a senior executive for a consumer goods corporation, and a military officer for the Reserve Component in Europe. When she decided to apply for an SES position, we transformed her Resumix into a senior-level federal resume package with full ECQ essays and a five-page SES resume.

Judy submitted her application against fierce competition. The Agency received approximately 117 applications for this coveted position, a position that would support the Agency's Secretary. Of the 117 applications, eight candidates were interviewed by a panel, in a structured interview environment with behavior-based questions. Of the eight who were interviewed, two were selected to interview with the Agency head. Judy was selected for the position and her ECQs were certified by the QRB.

Our focus was on highlighting her executive leadership across a diversity of organizations and describing powerful accomplishments, concentrating on the position description and Technical Qualifications. Keywords are in bold:

- Knowledge in **directing the development and implementation of new policies** for **Reserve readiness and training**

- Ability to **initiate programs, actions**, and **ensure adherence** to established **policies** and **national security objectives**

- Ability to **develop systems** and **standards** for the **administration of approved plans** and **programs**

- **Advisor to Agency head** and other senior stakeholders for **readiness, training, and operations, policy guidance, and program direction**

- Participate in **conducting analyses, providing guidance, making recommendations**, and **issuing guidance** for **defense plans and programs**

See also Judy Johnson's five-page resume
in Chapter 7 starting on page 119.

JUDY JOHNSON

Permanent: Judy@gmail.com
5420 Constantine Avenue   Cell: 555.202.4986
Washington, DC 92865
Announcement Number: SES-20XX, Executive Director, Mobilization & Training, Dept. of Navy

Major General, US Army Reserve   **05/2014 - Present**
Deputy Chief of Staff, Headquarters

Principal advisor to Commanding General, US Army Europe on all reserve component affairs and activities. Monitor processes for training and readiness of the Reserve components. Liaison between Commanding General, US Army Europe and Chief, Army Reserve and Director, Army National Guard for development of plans, policies and procedures for coordination and synchronization of Reserve Component integration into US Army Europe peacetime training support, as well as contingency operations.

US Army Reserve Components   **01/2012 - 05/2014**
Major General, US Army Reserve

Assisted Director, Strategic Plans in support of Chairman, Joint Chiefs of Staff top calendar issues. Served as Host Team Leader for Chemical Weapons Convention Challenge Inspections and annual challenge inspection exercises. Expert at annual NATO Crisis Management exercise. Represented the Office at international conferences, Joint Staff Talks, and other events.

Brigadier General, US Army Reserve   **07/2008 - 01/2012**
Commanding General, 3rd Army Reserve Command
Stuttgart, Germany

Led a major subordinate command of United States Army Europe, comprised of 34 units and 2,000 Reserve and Active-duty Soldiers, and civilian employees. Full accountability for ensuring subordinate units were manned, properly trained, and maintained a high rate of readiness for mobilization. Administered, planned, and executed an operating budget of ~$10M. Instituted a routine mobilization preparedness regimen for all units including enhanced measures in response to 9/11 to ensure personnel and unit mobilization readiness.

INDUSTRY EXPERIENCE

Executive Vice President, USA Region   **05/2006 - 05/2008**
Consumer Goods USA, Long Beach, CA

Implemented a strategic vision for business operations and development in the USA region of this international company with offices in 20 countries. Supervise large staff of 200+ including a sales force and plant workers, and independent distributors across five countries. Manage cross-cultural issues, enforce EEO regulations, and create programs to heighten morale and foster diversity. Manage a budget worth $7.9M.

Vice President, Corporate Marketing Initiatives　　　　　　**05/2004 - 05/2006**

Corporate-wide single point of contact for regulatory compliance and initiatives. Developed and implemented Direct Marketing vision, strategies, programs and budgets. Supervised 100+ staff and administered $47M marketing budget. Articulated instructions for Annual & Strategic Plan HQ instructions.

Accomplishments:
- Actively managed the Compliance Working Group in creating strategic and contingency plans for corporate response to regulatory trends. Ensured that financial and commercial impacts of directives were incorporated into Headquarters and individual market operating and strategic plans.
- Achieved the on-time, on-budget implementation of a corporate-wide consumer products directive. Compliance with the directive was named a corporate priority for the upcoming three-year period, as the out-year's corporate budget planning was already underway, and thus would have visibility with the Board of Directors.
- Heightened corporate acceptance of inevitable increased future regulation.
- Led implementation of corporate-wide Internet-based direct marketing pilot program.

Vice President, Imports　　　　　　　　　　　　　　　　**05/2002 - 05/2004**

Reported to Regional President as member of Regional Executive Committee. Supervised staff of 28. Managed all aspects of importation of sales of high-margin brands into the USA.

Accomplishments:
- Successfully disengaged from importers, thwarting importer strategy of multi-million dollar cash extraction and disturbance of commercial operations.

Earlier Employment History
- General Manager, Consumer Products, USA, 2000 - 2002
    Complete P&L responsibility for more than $100M in domestic sales, distribution and marketing of products manufactured in two local factories and imported from the USA, plus export sales to European countries. Reported to Regional President.

EDUCATION
- Master of Business Administration, University of Maryland, 2003
- Bachelor of Science in International Relations, University of Virginia, 1993
- National Security Management Course, National Defense University, 2014
- US Army Command and General Staff Officer Course, 2013

We worked with Judy to develop a list of top ten major career accomplishments and leadership initiatives, focused on the ECQs and TQs from the announcement. From this list, we drafted full ECQ essays. (We did not draft CCAR stories for Judy in the below examples, as we did for Keith Smith, Case Study #2 beginning on page 107.) To finalize the package, we wove short summary versions of the ECQ essays into the five-page SES resume. Here is the top ten list, describing Judy's diverse career:

1. **Improved morale with new leadership team (Leading People)**

    Led a diverse headquarters' staff in Long Beach composed of personnel from two U.S. regions, the Headquarters, and members from two countries. This comprised the management team and the mid-level staff. The management team handled their direct-reports in a very hierarchical, depreciative manner, resulting in many complaints and personnel turbulence. Under my guidance, I introduced team-building requirements and the staff showed markedly improved morale and reduced personnel turbulence.

2. **Analyzed trends among regions and led change to incorporate 10-year assessment of trends (Leading Change)**

    Developed, agreed upon, and implemented a strategic vision for Consumer Goods USA's business operations across the nation and the plants in 20 other countries to standardize operations reflecting 5- to 10-year assessment of regional trends including Free Trade Agreements; market regulatory trends; trade evolution; and competitive strategies. Incorporated relevant elements into annual and strategic business objectives, plans, programs and budgets, including organizational and business mode shifts.

3. **Led Regulatory Compliance Group (Business Acumen)**

    Actively managed the Regulatory Compliance Working Group in creating strategic and contingency plans for corporate response to regulatory trends. Ensured that financial and commercial impacts of directives were incorporated into Headquarters and individual market operating and strategic plans. Led the implementation of an Internet-based direct marketing pilot program which was rolled out across the corporation.

4. **Business turnaround after hemorrhaging cash (Business Acumen)**

    Turned around a business unit that had been hemorrhaging cash for previous two years. Rallied organization behind vision statement. Closed two plants. Controlled imports of high-margin premium brands.

5.   **Oversaw two major Joint Army and Air Force Exercises, Special Operations Forces** (Leading People)

Oversaw two major Army and Air Force exercises. Led a multi-service staff team and multiple Army and Marine organizations in planning and execution as part of a U.S.-led Joint Task Force operating in a sovereign host nation. Determined the forces required for both combat and post-combat phases; set the theater for port, airfield and basing needs; coordinated flow in and staging of forces and materiel.

6.   **Exercise Director, Foreign Consequence Management Exercises** (Building Coalitions)

Exercise Director and principal advisor for U.S. Army Europe Foreign Consequence Management exercises, which tested the ability of U.S. Army Europe and U.S. European Command to respond to foreign chemical, biological, radiological and nuclear incidents, in coordination with the U.S. Department of State and host nation ministries of interior and indigenous consequence management forces.

7.   **USAR Schools Initiative** (Results Driven)

Spearheaded U.S. Army Reserve (USAR) Schools Initiative in Europe, increasing interoperability by teaching U.S. military doctrine to foreign military partners and the U.S. interagency.

8.   **Selected as Deputy Chief of Staff, Operations for several months** (Results Driven)

Oversight leadership for 1,200 Soldiers and civilians and 21 divisions, supporting war plans, training, exercises and international operations for 70,000 Soldiers in U.S. Army Europe; as well as the deployment and redeployment of U.S. Army Europe units and individuals to Iraq and Afghanistan for Operations Enduring Freedom and Iraqi Freedom.

9.   **Consolidated units into Reserve Centers** (Results Driven)

Achieved greater return on investment in facilities and automation infrastructure, as well as synergies in administration and training.

10.   **Principal advisor to Commanding General, U.S. Army Europe** (Technical Qualification & Building Coalitions)

Advisor to senior leadership for all Reserve Component affairs, activities, and policy development in region. Monitor processes for training and readiness; serve as liaison between numerous stakeholder organizations for the development of plans, policies, and procedures for coordination and synchronization of Reserve Component integration into U.S. Army Europe peacetime training support, as well as contingency operations.

JUDY JOHNSON

Permanent:
5420 Constantine Avenue, Washington, DC 92865

Judy@gmail.com
Cell: 555.202.4986

Citizenship: U.S.
Announcement Number: SES-20XX, Executive Director, Mobilization & Training, Dept. of Navy

EXECUTIVE PROFILE

Major General, U.S. Army (Active & Reserve), 20-year career
15-year Corporate Career / Senior Sales and Marketing Executive
Multi-lingual: German & French | TS/SCI

Senior executive with full oversight direction for strategic planning and business leadership for large, geographically separated organizations, hundreds of employees and multi-million dollar operating budgets, while holding dual careers with multi-national, fast-moving consumer goods corporations, and in leading U.S. Army organizations. Develop policy and regulatory compliance. Culturally acclimatized, politically correct, and diplomatic; excellent political-military skills. Structure joint operations.

• • •

U.S. Army (Active & Reserve Components) Experience, 1995 - Present

Major General, U.S. Army Reserve (Active Duty)
Deputy Chief of Staff, Washington, DC and Headquarters Europe
Supervisor: John Jones; 555.398.3800; Contact: Yes

05/2014 - Present
Hours per week: 40
Salary: $150K per year

Principal advisor to Commanding General (Director-equivalent), U.S. Army Europe on all Reserve component affairs, activities, and policy development. Monitor processes for training and readiness of the Reserve Components to meet security and force protection objectives. Liaison between Commanding General, U.S. Army Europe and Chief, Army Reserve and Director, Army National Guard for development of plans, policies, procedures, and guidance for coordination and synchronization of Reserve Components integration into U.S. Army Europe peacetime training support, as well as contingency operations. Represent leadership at exercises, conferences and other activities involving Reserve Component personnel and issues, to include distinguished visitors to the U.S. Army Europe area of responsibility.

Key Leadership Initiatives:
- Oversaw two major Army and Air Force exercises. Led a multi-service staff and multiple Army and Marine organizations in planning and execution as part of a U.S.-led Joint Task Force operating in a sovereign host nation. Guided senior staff in determining the personnel strength required for both combat and post-combat phases; setting the Theater for port, airfield and basing needs; coordinating flow in and staging of forces and materiel; conducting ground combat operations, synchronizing with Air Force, Navy and Special Operations Forces counterparts; managing immediate post-combat stability and humanitarian relief operations, as well as redeployment of U.S. forces and transition of the land forces mission to the host nation and international organizations. **(Leading People/Results Driven/Business Acumen)**
  - As a result of successful performance, appointed Deputy Exercise Director for the next Fiscal Year's major exercise, which entails mentoring an active component major general (senior level) and leading the ground force activities of the Joint Exercise Control Group. **(Leading People)**

- Deputy Chief of Staff, Operations, U.S. Army Europe for several months. Oversight leadership for 1,200 military personnel and civilians and 21 divisions, supporting war plans, training, exercises and international operations for 70,000 Soldiers in U.S. Army Europe; as well as the deployment and redeployment of U.S. Army Europe units and individuals to Iraq and Afghanistan for Operations Enduring Freedom and Iraqi Freedom. **(Results Driven)**
- Exercise Director for U.S. Army Europe Foreign Consequence Management exercises, which test the ability of U.S. Army Europe and U.S. European Command to respond to foreign chemical, biological, radiological and nuclear incidents, in coordination with the U.S. Department of State and host nation ministries of interior and indigenous consequence management forces. **(Building Coalitions)**
- Spearheaded U.S. Army Reserve (USAR) Schools Initiative in U.S. Army Europe, increasing interoperability by teaching U.S. military doctrine to foreign military partners and the U.S. interagency. **(Results Driven)**

Major General, U.S. Army Reserve (Active Duty)	**05/2012 - 05/2014**
Deputy Director Planning, the Pentagon, Washington, DC	**Hours per week: 40**
Supervisor: Jerry Winters; 555.497.4488; Contact: Yes	**Salary: $150K per year**

Advised Director, Strategic Plans in support of Chairman, Joint Chiefs of Staff top calendar issues for defense plans and programs. Served as Host Team Leader for Chemical Weapons Convention Challenge Inspections and annual challenge inspection exercises. Expert at annual NATO Crisis Management exercise. Represented the Organization and top leadership at international conferences, Joint Staff Talks, and other events.

Key Leadership Initiatives:
- Senior U.S. military representative at U.S. Department of State-led conferences and negotiations: Organization for Security and Cooperation in Europe, Proliferation Security Initiative, and EUCOM-sponsored conference for the Economic Union Of West African States. At Proliferation Security Initiative conference, participated in negotiations with Russian contingent to achieve tangible commitments to this critical undertaking. **(Building Coalitions)**
- Conducted diplomatic negotiations gaining respect of allied hosts. Directly contributed to Mexico's decision to begin Joint Staff Talks; led the annual Joint Staff Talks with Chile. **(Building Coalitions)**

Brigadier General, U.S. Army Reserve (Active Duty)	**05/2008 - 05/2012**
3rd Army Reserve Command, Germany	**Hours per week: 40**
Supervisor: Andrew K. Myers; 555.202.2002; Contact: Yes	**Salary: $150K per year**

Led a major subordinate organization of United States Army Europe, composed of 34 units and 2,000 Reserve and Active-duty Soldiers, and civilian employees. Full accountability for ensuring subordinate units were manned, properly trained, and maintained a high rate of readiness for mobilization. Administered, planned, and executed an operating budget of $30M. Recommended and instituted a routine mobilization preparedness regimen, and associated issuing guidance, for all units including enhanced measures in response to 9/11 to ensure personnel and unit mobilization readiness across the organization.

Key Leadership Initiatives:
- Realigned force structure to meet the evolving needs of the total Army. Initiated an annual force structure review process with HQ U.S. Army Europe (USAREUR) and its major subordinate commands. **(Leading Change)**

- Guided implementation of Equipment Storage Site-Expanded concept, producing a validated 97% equipment serviceability rate from previous 75%, in just one year. Outsourced logistics, increasing by 25% the time for units to focus precious training time on their core competency: mission operations. **(Results Driven)**
- Consolidated units into Reserve Centers, achieving greater return on investment in facilities and automation infrastructure, as well as synergies in administration and training. **(Leading Change/Results Driven)**
- Conducted negotiations with German Federal defense and finance ministries, gained HQ U.S. Army Europe support, and achieved NATO "member of the force" status for the organization's drilling Reservists, thereby providing them the same PX and commissary access as Reserve Soldiers in the USA. **(Building Coalitions/Results Driven)**

Previous Military Assignments (Reserve Duty)
- **7th U.S. Army Reserve Command**, Deputy Chief of Staff Operations, Chief of Staff in HQs. Various command and staff positions at subordinate units, Germany, 1998 to 2008
- **Army National Guard**, Liaison Officer 42nd Division Artillery, New York, 1995 to 2004

Consumer Goods USA, 15-YEAR INDUSTRY CAREER

Executive Vice President	**05/2006 - 05/2008**
Long Beach, CA	**Hours per week: 40**
Supervisor: Mr. Tom Hansen; 555.349.2940; Contact: Yes	**Salary: $150K per year**

* Consumer Goods USA is an international consumer goods business with 25,000 employees in 20 countries.

Implemented a strategic vision for business operations and development in the USA region of this international company with offices in 20 countries. Indirectly supervise an office staff of 65 and sales force of 80, with dotted-line supervision to 175 plant workers, and independent distributors across five countries. I manage cross-cultural issues, enforce EEO regulations, and create programs to heighten morale and foster diversity. Manage an operational budget worth $7.9M.

Key Leadership Initiatives:
- Integrated the brands, employees, distributors and business operations of a major company acquisition in 2009. **(Business Acumen)**
- Achieved annual and strategic plan (3-year planning horizon) volume and profit targets. **(Results Driven)**
- Empowered and coached a diverse staff with low morale; gained trust and energized a very talented management team and their direct-reports to exceed their potential. Led a headquarters' staff in Long Beach composed of personnel from two U.S. regions, the Headquarters, and members from two counties. This comprised the management team and the mid-level staff. The management team handled their direct-reports in a very hierarchical, depreciative manner, resulting in many complaints and personnel turbulence. To establish the new leadership team, I scheduled an off-site meeting and directed that the meeting be prepared and conducted by the new leadership team, who presented their proposals to management. This successful meeting institutionalized the new leadership construct and I achieved a leadership culture of inclusion, empowerment, and teamwork. The HQ staff showed markedly improved morale and reduced personnel turbulence. **(Leading People)**

- Ensured full integration of new plant in Long Beach. Melded marketing and sales organization from east coast for office support (Finance, IT, Logistics, Legal & HR) and ensured cooperation between HQ marketing and sales departments, HQ R&D and Global Supply Chain. **(Building Coalitions)**
- Developed, agreed upon, and implemented a strategic vision for Consumer Products USA's business operations across the nation and the plants in 20 other countries to standardize operations reflecting 5- to 10-year assessment of regional trends including Free Trade Agreements; market regulatory trends; trade evolution; and competitive strategies. Incorporated relevant elements into annual and strategic business objectives, plans, programs and budgets, including organizational and business mode shifts. **(Leading Change)**

Vice President, Corporate Marketing Initiatives   05/2004 - 05/2006
Cincinnati, Ohio   Hours per week: 40
Supervisor: Mr. Donald Anderson: 495.874.9230; Contact: Yes   Salary: $150K per year

Corporate-wide single point of contact for corporate marketing and regulatory compliance and initiatives. Developed and implemented Direct Marketing vision, strategies, programs and budgets. Supervised 100+ staff and administered $47M marketing budget. Articulated Regulatory market instructions for Annual & Strategic Plan HQ instructions.

Key Leadership Initiatives:
- Formed and actively managed the Regulatory Compliance Working Group in creating strategic and contingency plans for corporate response to regulatory trends. Ensured that financial and commercial impacts of directives were incorporated into Headquarters and individual market operating and strategic plans. **(Business Acumen)**
- Guided development of and achieved the on-time, on-budget implementation of a corporate-wide consumer products directive, which saved the company $45 million over five years. Compliance with the directive was named a corporate priority for the upcoming three-year period, as the out-year's corporate budget planning was already underway, and thus would have visibility with the Board of Directors. **(Results Driven)**
- Led implementation of corporate-wide Internet-based direct marketing pilot program, which was so successful that is was adopted corporate-wide and expanded to cell phone coverage and social media. **(Business Acumen)**

Vice President, Imports   05/2002 - 05/2004
Long Beach, CA   Hours per week: 40
Supervisor: Mr. James Smith; 555.349.7811; Contact: Yes   Salary: $150K per year

Reported to Regional President as member of Regional Executive Committee. Supervised senior staff of 28. Managed all aspects of importation of $70M sales of high-margin premium and sub-premium brands from five countries.

Key Leadership Initiatives:
- Successfully disengaged from importers, thwarting importer strategy of multi-million dollar cash extraction and disturbance of commercial operations. **(Business Acumen)**

- Directed multi-functional team of operations in five countries: R&D, HQ packaging, plant, and marketing and sales staff to ensure synchronized product, packaging, operations planning, marketing and selling activities. **(Leading People)**
- Secured return of bank guarantees of $28 million via successful negotiations with foreign customs authorities, as well as rigorous project management of simultaneous product disposal and excise stamp recovery operations in two major cities. **(Business Acumen)**
- Successfully redeployed key managers via intensive personal networking, as well as coaching/mentoring and exposure via delegating direct responsibility for projects. **(Leading People)**

Earlier Position

General Manager, Consumer Goods USA, 2000 - 2002 (Long Beach, CA)

Complete P&L responsibility for more than $100M in domestic sales, distribution and marketing of products manufactured in two local plants and imported from five countries. Reported to Regional President. Directly supervised 19 director-level staff and office staff of 60 at the HQ office. Oversight direction for 120-strong field sales force and 2,000 plant employees across the USA.

- Turned around a business that had been hemorrhaging cash for previous two years. Rallied organization behind vision statement. Achieved control of imports of high-margin premium brands formerly managed by Export Department. Instituted sales/marketing programs to fully align and motivate staff and sales force and trade behind the newfound Total Brand Portfolio Management. Closed two plants, securing $12M in cost savings. **(Business Acumen)**

EDUCATION & U.S. ARMY PROFESSIONAL MILITARY EDUCATION

- Master of Business Administration, University of Maryland, 2003
- Bachelor of Science in International Relations, University of Virginia, 1993
- National Security Management Course, National Defense University, 2014
- U.S. Army Command and General Staff Officer Course, 2013

PUBLIC SPEAKING ENGAGEMENTS

- "U.S. Army Europe in Transformation." Delivered speech in German, 2015
- American Chamber of Commerce Serbia, and Serbian and international press. "Update on International Operations and Investments in Serbia," Serbia, 2014
- Press conference, UN Palace of Nations, Geneva, Switzerland, 2013
- Conferences / Symposia
- Annual Serbia and Albania Economist Intelligence Unit conferences, 2008 - present
- First Annual Proliferation Security Initiative Conference, Warsaw, Poland, 2011

OTHER

Languages: German 3/3 • French 3/3

Military Awards & Decorations: Legion of Merit • Defense Meritorious Service Medal • Meritorious Service Medal • Army Commendation Medal • Army Achievement Medal

Clearance: TS/SCI

SOME AGENCIES REQUIRE THE RESUME TO BE IN THE USAJOBS RESUME BUILDER. The builder executive resume version should be in the **OUTLINE FORMAT with ALL CAP KEYWORDS** as seen here, to help the Executive Resources HR Recruiter identify key leadership competencies and technical qualifications required from the vacancy announcement. *Note: USAJOBS automatically orders the employment sections by dates, and Judy's industry experience is mixed with the military service by date order.

THE PAPER EXECUTIVE RESUME at about five pages, does not need to be in the outline format with all caps. It provides the same profile information and same functional category headers, with shorter accomplishment bullets than the five-page resume-based application. The short accomplishment bullets will be more fully addressed in the CCAR format in the ECQ and TQ essays that accompany the executive federal resume.

JUDY JOHNSON
5420 Constantine Avenue
Washington, DC 92865
Day Phone: 555.202.4986
Email: Judy@gmail.com

WORK EXPERIENCE: U.S. Army Europe (Active Duty)   **5/2014 - Present**
                         The Pentagon & Germany
                         Salary: $150,000 USD Per Year
                         Hours per week: 40

DEPUTY CHIEF OF STAFF (MAJOR GENERAL), HEADQUARTERS
PRINCIPAL ADVISOR TO COMMANDING GENERAL, U.S. Army Europe on all Reserve component affairs and activities. Monitor processes for training and readiness of the Reserve components. Liaison between multiple military components for development of plans, policies, and procedures for training support and contingency operations. Oversight leadership for 1,200 Soldiers and civilians and 21 divisions. Organizational representative at meetings, events, and exercises. Unique additional leadership oversight includes:

KEY ACCOMPLISHMENTS:

OPERATIONS MANAGEMENT: Led two major Army and Air Force exercises. Supervised and guided a multi-service staff team and multiple Army and Marine organizations in planning and execution as part of a U.S.-led Joint Task Force operating in a sovereign host nation.

EXECUTIVE MENTORSHIP: Appointed Deputy Exercise Director for the next Fiscal Year's major exercise, which entails mentoring an active component major general (senior officer) and leading the ground force activities of the Joint Exercise Control Group.

TRAINING PROGRAM: Spearheaded USAR Schools Initiative in Europe, increasing interoperability by teaching U.S. military doctrine to foreign military partners.

(Contact Supervisor: Yes, Supervisor's Name: John Jones, Supervisor's Phone: 555.398.3800)

U.S. Army Reserve (Active Duty)   **05/2012 - 05/2014**
Washington, DC US
Salary: $150,000 USD Per Year
Hours per week: 40

DEPUTY DIRECTOR PLANNING, MAJOR GENERAL, U.S. ARMY RESERVE

ASSISTED DIRECTOR, STRATEGIC PLANS IN SUPPORT OF CHAIRMAN, JOINT CHIEFS of Staff top calendar issues. Expert at annual NATO Crisis Management exercise. Represented the Office at international conferences, Joint Staff Talks, and other events.

KEY ACCOMPLISHMENTS:

COMMUNICATIONS: Senior U.S. military representative at U.S. Department of State-led conferences and negotiations. At Proliferation Security Initiative conference, participated in negotiations with foreign contingent to achieve tangible commitments to this critical undertaking.

JOINT NEGOTIATIONS: Guided diplomatic negotiations gaining respect of allied hosts. Directly contributed to Mexico's decision to begin Joint Staff Talks; led the annual Joint Staff Talks with Chile.

PROCEDURES DEVELOPMENT: Developed first-ever Host Team Leader brief delineating Host Team activities that were synchronized with pre-established inspection timelines. This brief was incorporated into Host Team standard procedures.

(Contact Supervisor: Yes, Supervisor's Name: Jerry Winters, Supervisor's Phone: 555.497.4488)

Commanding General, 3rd Army Reserve Command
05/2008 - 05/2012
Germany
Salary: $150,000 USD Per Year
Hours per week: 40

BRIGADIER GENERAL (CEO-equivalent), U.S. ARMY RESERVE (Active Duty)

LED A MAJOR SUBORDINATE COMMAND of United States Army Europe, composed of 34 units and 2,000 Reserve and Active-duty Soldiers, and civilian employees. Administered and executed an operating budget of ~$30M. Supervised 15 direct report subordinate managers.

OPERATIONS MANAGEMENT: Fully accountable for ensuring subordinate units were manned, trained, and maintained a high rate of readiness for mobilization.

KEY ACCOMPLISHMENTS:

PROCEDURES DEVELOPMENT: Realigned force structure to meet the evolving needs of the total Army. Initiated an annual force structure review process with HQ and its major subordinate commands.

PROGRAM DEVELOPMENT AND LEADERSHIP: Instituted a routine mobilization preparedness regimen for all units including enhanced measures in response to 9/11 to ensure personnel and unit mobilization readiness.

EQUIPMENT MANAGEMENT: IMPLEMENTED EQUIPMENT STORAGE SITE-EXPANDED CONCEPT, producing a validated 97% equipment serviceability rate from previous 75%, in just one year.

LOGISTICS MANAGEMENT: Outsourced logistics, increasing by 25% the time for units to focus precious training time on their core competency: mission operations.

(Contact Supervisor: Yes, Supervisor's Name: Andrew K. Myers, Supervisor's Phone: 202.555.2002)

Consumer Goods USA International 05/2006 – 05/2008
Long Beach, CA
Salary: 150,000 USD Per Year
Hours per week: 40

EXECUTIVE VICE PRESIDENT

Consumer Goods USA is a consumer goods business with 25,000 employees in 40 countries across the globe.

LEADERSHIP OVERSIGHT FOR IMPLEMENTING A STRATEGIC VISION for business development and operations in the USA region of this international company. Supervised 65 office staff, 80 field sales personnel, and provided dotted-line supervision to 175 plant workers, and independent distributors across five countries. Managed an operational budget worth $7.9M. Incorporated relevant elements into annual and strategic business objectives, plans, programs and budgets, including organizational and business mode shifts.

PERSONNEL ADMINISTRATION: Managed cross-cultural issues, enforced EEO regulations, and created programs to heighten morale and foster diversity. Empowered and coached staff with low morale, gained trust, and energized a very talented management team and their direct reports to exceed their potential.

KEY ACCOMPLISHMENTS:

ACQUISITION MANAGEMENT: Integrated the brands, employees, distributors, and business operations of a major company acquisition.
BUSINESS DEVELOPMENT: Achieved annual and strategic plan (3-year planning horizon) volume and profit targets.

FACTORY INTEGRATION: Ensured full integration of new plant in Long Beach. Melded marketing and sales organization from east coast for office support (Finance, IT, Logistics, Legal & HR) and ensured cooperation between HQ marketing and sales departments, HQ R&D and Global Supply Chain.

(Contact Supervisor: Yes, Supervisor's Name: Tom Hansen, Supervisor's Phone: 555-349-2940)

Consumer Goods USA   **05/2004 - 05/2006**
Cincinnati, OH
Salary: $140,000 USD Per Year
Hours per week: 40

VICE PRESIDENT, CORPORATE MARKETING INITIATIVES

CORPORATE-WIDE SINGLE POINT OF CONTACT for regulatory compliance and initiatives. Developed and implemented Direct Marketing vision, strategies, programs and budgets. Supervisor of 100+ staff. Administered $47M marketing budget. Articulated Regulatory market instructions for Annual & Strategic Plan HQ instructions.

KEY ACCOMPLISHMENTS:

COALITION BUILDING: Actively managed the Regulatory Compliance Working Group in creating strategic and contingency plans for corporate response to regulatory trends.

PROJECT MANAGEMENT: Guided development of and achieved the on-time, on-budget implementation of a corporate-wide consumer products directive, which saved the company $45 million over five years.

TECHNOLOGY INTEGRATION: Led implementation of corporate-wide Internet-based direct marketing pilot program.

(Contact Supervisor: Yes, Supervisor's Name: Donald Anderson, Supervisor's Phone: 49.555.874.9230)

Consumer Goods USA   05/2002 - 05/2004
Long Beach, CA
Salary: $105,000 USD Per Year
Hours per week: 40

VICE PRESIDENT, IMPORTS

OVERSIGHT SUPERVISION FOR SENIOR STAFF of 28. Directed multi-functional team of operations in five countries. Managed all aspects of importation of $70M sales of high-margin premium and sub-premium brands. Reported to Regional President as member of Regional Executive Committee.

KEY ACCOMPLISHMENTS:

NEGOTIATIONS: Successfully negotiated and managed disengagement from importers, thwarting importer strategy of multi-million dollar cash extraction and disturbance of commercial operations.

PROJECT MANAGEMENT: Managed full project management lifecycle of multi-functional operations team for plant R&D, HQ Packaging, and marketing & sales staff to ensure synchronized Product, Packaging, Operations Planning, Marketing and Selling activities.

INTERNATIONAL FINANCE: Secured return of bank guarantees of $28 million via successful negotiations with Russian customs authorities.

(Contact Supervisor: Yes, Supervisor's Name: James Smith, Supervisor's Phone: 555.349.7811)

EDUCATION: University of Maryland
                          College Park, MD US
                          Master's Degree - 5/2003
                          Major: Masters in Business Administration

                          University of Virginia
                          Charlottesville, VA US
                          Bachelor's Degree - 6/1993
                          Major: International Relations

                          National Defense University
                          Washington, DC US
                          Some College Coursework Completed, 2013
                          Major: National Security Management Course

PROFESSIONAL PUBLICATIONS:

PUBLIC SPEAKING ENGAGEMENTS AND WRITTEN PRESENTATIONS:

- "U.S. Army Europe in Transformation". Delivered speech in German, 2015
- American Chamber of Commerce Serbia, and Serbian and international press. "Update on International Operations and Investments in Serbia", Serbia, 2014
- Press conference, UN Palace of Nations, Geneva, Switzerland, 2013

Conferences / Symposia
- Annual Serbia and Albania Economist Intelligence Unit conferences, 2008 - present
- First Annual Proliferation Security Initiative Conference, Warsaw, Poland, 2011

ADDITIONAL INFORMATION:

EXECUTIVE PROFILE

- 15-year Corporate Career / Senior Sales & Marketing Executive / Consumer Goods USA
- Major General, U.S. Army Reserve (1995 - present)
- Multi-lingual: German & French
- TS/SCI

Senior executive with full oversight direction for strategic planning and business leadership for large, geographically separated organizations, hundreds of employees and multi-million dollar operating budgets, while holding dual careers with multi-national, fast-moving consumer goods corporations, and in leading U.S. Army organizations. Develop policy and regulatory compliance. Culturally acclimatized, politically correct, and diplomatic; excellent political-military skills. Structure joint operations.

Previous Military Assignments (Reserve Duty)

- 7th U.S. Army Reserve Command, Deputy Chief of Staff Operations, Chief of Staff in HQs. Various command and staff positions at subordinate units, Germany, 1998 to 2008

- Army National Guard, Liaison Officer 42nd Division Artillery, New York, 1995 to 2004

Business Acumen

As the Vice President of Corporate Marketing Initiatives Consumer Goods USA, at the headquarters in Geneva, Switzerland, I led the implementation of an Internet-based direct marketing pilot program, which was rolled-out corporate-wide. With ever-increasing restrictions on the tobacco industry, it became difficult to communicate with consumers of the company's products. **(Challenge)**

There was a clearly articulated intention for a complete advertising and promotion ban on tobacco products by European Union (EU) parliament when it passed the EU Tobacco Products Directive (including health warnings and tar-nicotine-carbon monoxide labeling on cigarette packaging). Similar intentions were articulated by consumer advocate organizations (e.g., World Health Organization). Corporate senior leadership's inclination was to not invest in programs with future benefits where the exact timing of regulation could not be specified. There was a growing general culture of complacency concerning the inevitability of ever-more restrictive legislation on tobacco products. **(Context)**

At the time, there was also an exponential increase in PC penetration and e-commerce in Western Europe. I was thus challenged to convince corporate leadership to leverage technology and develop an e-marketing program while it was still possible to gather consumer data via traditional on-pack and retail promotion vehicles. Taking action, I led development of very effective and successful e-marketing informational and promotional programs that effectively reached consumers and built the business among the company's franchise, and attracted competitors' consumers. **(Action)**

I developed the strategic vision to substantially increase the company's (HQ and markets) direct marketing capability over the annual and strategic planning (AP/SP) two-year period. Additionally, I led outside consultants to deliver a menu for key markets of e-marketing consumer communication systems, I managed the market-focused conditions-setting phase, and I devised detailed plans, programs and budget for the AP/SP out-years. **(Action)**

Then, I oversaw development of the e-marketing program working alongside the IT and social medial departments, which included effective use of social medial platforms (Facebook, Twitter, YouTube, Google ads, and email campaigns); and I collaborated with the Chief Financial Officer to develop the budget for selected pilot markets, and for corporate-wide implementation upon pilot market success. **(Action)**

Once securing Board approval, I guided the consultants and rallied pilot market general managers to dedicate sales and marketing personnel and promotional budgets to e-marketing efforts. The pilot programs were successfully initiated in three European markets and then in six regions in the USA. With these results, the e-marketing project institutionalized and was handed-off to the sales department for corporate-wide implementation. **(Results)**

Results Driven

As U.S. Host Team Leader for Chemical Weapons Convention Challenge Inspections, which were exercised annually, I had to make improvements on a flawed structural concept. While the Host Team and I acquitted ourselves reasonably well on the first challenge inspection exercise, I by no means felt that the Host Team was as effective as it could be and certainly did not respond to the Inspection Team to the required degree. The Host Team never formed as a team, as it was in a crisis reaction mode during the entire inspection period. Members were not conversant in the challenge inspection procedures or published draft Department of Defense guidance. Even more disappointing, the after-action review comments mirrored those of the previous three years' challenge inspections, indicating that lessons-learned were not being implemented by those charged with advancing the art between challenge inspection exercises. I was determined to redress this unsatisfactory condition on the next challenge inspection exercise the following year. **(Challenge)**

The Host Team is an ad hoc organization comprised of senior multi-service and interagency members led by a Flag Officer (senior officer) Host Team Leader, all of whom are designated only when a challenge inspection notification is delivered to the United States. Any signatory of the Convention for the Prevention of Chemical Weapons that suspects another member is in violation of the convention can request a challenge inspection to be conducted by technically proficient inspectors from the Office of the Prevention of Chemical Weapons in The Hague, the Netherlands. The Host Team must begin interaction with the Inspection Team within 24 hours of arrival of the Office for Prevention of Chemical Weapons Inspection Team. While assigned to the Strategic Plans and Policy Directorate (J-5) of the Joint Staff (US Army, The Pentagon), I was designated as Host Team Leader. **(Context)**

Taking action to resolve these serious problems and provide accountability to all stakeholders, I recognized that I needed to become a subject matter expert on the Chemical Weapons Convention Challenge Inspection regimen in order to effectively and credibly lead the Host Team and, equally important, to institute needed changes in existing, unsatisfactory Host Team procedures. I immersed myself in the Chemical Weapons Convention and Defense Threat Reduction Agency training material, becoming fluent in the challenge of inspection requirements and timelines. I developed a presentation that outlined challenge inspection procedure and timelines, as well as the protocols that the Host Team would follow. **(Actions)**

Challenge inspections typically began with the Host Team meeting together for the first time only one hour prior to the arrival of the Inspection Team. I realized that the only time available for me to form the team under my leadership and indoctrinate it to the challenge inspection requirements was in the 24 hours after the Host Team members were designated, prior to arrival of the Inspection Team at the port of embarkation and receipt of their initial Host Team briefing. I convened a meeting of the Host Team immediately following its designation and presented my vision of Host Team operations. I addressed my overall approach to managing the challenge inspection, delineated Executive Secretariat roles and responsibilities, and very specifically defined Host Team activities from the first meeting at the port of embarkation to the first meeting at the inspected installation. **(Actions)**

Host Team operations improved compared to the previous exercise. The Host Team noticeably transitioned to a more deliberate, anticipatory and proactive approach to challenge inspection requirements and Inspection Team requests and issues. The Inspection Team was led and challenged by a Host Team that was more proficient and responsive. The final after action report's major findings and recommendations cited my Host Team pre-meeting and presentation as a first-ever event that was both innovative and highly successful, and recommended that it be adopted as the standard for a Host Team Leader initial presentation. **(Results)**

Executive Cover Letter

A cover letter or letter of interest may accompany a senior executive application package to help a candidate stand out. Make sure to follow carefully the vacancy announcement requirements; some agencies request the inclusion of a cover letter with an SES application package, while other agencies indicate that they will only accept a resume or other specified documents, and will not review any documents beyond those specified.

The purpose of a cover letter is to describe the applicant's interest in the position and to reemphasize qualifications consistent with the vacancy announcement; it should not simply restate the content of the resume. If the letter is written well, the HR staff will glean prominent qualifications from your application that are most critical to the advertised position, and you may build some rapport with the reader. Leverage the cover letter to highlight brief examples of how your experience is a strong fit for the position, and to illuminate convincing leadership qualifications essential to the open position. Structure the cover letter to help you stand out among even the fiercest competition.

The cover letter components may include:

1. **A header** that matches the header of a formatted federal resume. Preparing a standard header that can be used for all of your presentation resumes, cover letters, ECQ essays, and other documents will create a theme and a professional appearance.

2. **Short leadership highlights or bullet points** to affirm information contained within the resume/application. Bullets points break up the page and help the reader's eye to zero in on specific achievements or points of interest.

3. **An explanation of transferable skill sets** if you feel you are only minimally qualified in a leadership or technical competency. For example, if you are experienced in all ECQs and TQs, but lack specific knowledge of an agency-specific regulation, yet you are familiar with an equivalent regulation from your agency or company, then you may use the cover letter to describe the equivalent level of knowledge and how it might translate to the target agency.

It is important to personalize and address each cover letter to the individual listed on the vacancy announcement. Be certain to identify the announcement number, position title, and a list of attachments for each application. Each letter should be concise, targeted to a specific position, energetic, and positive, and it should describe to the reader the executive contributions you can make.

The cover letter can be one to one and a half pages, with one-inch margins and the same font used for the resume (12-point font). The cover letter may be uploaded to USAJOBS or Application Manager (as a formatted Word document), as needed, or used as an email attachment or hard copy. For online systems, you will want to convert the cover letter content to a text file and copy and paste it into the appropriate federal builder. Follow the instructions for specific character lengths.

JUDY JOHNSON

Permanent:
5420 Constantine Avenue, Washington, DC 92865

Judy@gmail.com
Cell: 555.202.4986

Date

Susan Smith, HR Director
Dept. of Navy Mobilization & Training
The Pentagon, Washington, DC 22210

Announcement Number: SES-20xx, Executive Director, Mobilization & Training, Department of Navy

Dear Ms. Smith and Executive Review Panel:

Enclosed is my executive resume, ECQs, and TQs for the position of Executive Director, Mobilization & Training, Dept. of Navy.

I offer a rare blend of senior leadership from within industry and from serving as an officer for the U.S. Army Reserve. My policy and military regulatory compliance development, financial management, personnel administration and management of large workforces around the globe, and corporate experience, complemented by broad operational skills in mobilization, deployment, training, readiness, and logistics and top-tier client relationship management, is a solid fit with the Executive Director position.

Throughout my career, I have proven my ability in building productive teams, applying a direct communication style, advising senior leaders and stakeholders, and making recommendations and issuing guidance for defense plans and programs, as well as building sustainable programs delivering replicable results for industry.

As the representative of my organization at international conferences, I am comfortable speaking to all echelons and responding to questions concerning training and mobilization of forces overseas, serving as a subject matter expert and authority. I excel at policy development and implementation, and negotiating challenging issues with foreign nationals delivering positive results. Additionally, as a military officer, I seek to continue to support the military through this government position.

If these qualities and experiences might enhance your organizational mission, I will be pleased to make myself available for an interview to describe my capabilities as a senior leader and how I can benefit your agency with my credentials. Thank you for your consideration.

Sincerely,

Judy Johnson

Enclosure: Resume

Chapter Seven

The Five-Page SES Federal Resume

Creating Your Five-Page SES Federal Resume

Your challenge in writing the five-page resume will be to describe up to 20 years of experience and include evidence of the ECQs and required TQs in the text of the resume. The final product will be a coherent five-page document that tells a story of senior leadership by covering all 28 leadership competencies, but not actually identifying the ECQ categories. The 2012 Guide to SES Qualifications by OPM states: "Candidates should keep the ECQs in mind as they write their resumes, but it is not necessary or even advisable to annotate the resume with 'Leading Change', 'Leading People', 'Results Driven', 'Business Acumen', or 'Building Coalitions'" ECQ labels in the SES resume samples in this book are for reference only.

The evaluators are looking for demonstrated evidence of your ECQs and the leadership competencies woven throughout the entire five pages.

Page 1 of a Five-Page SES Federal Resume in USAJOBS, Emphasizing ECQ Accomplishments

THEODORE ROOSEVELT

WORK EXPERIENCE

United States of America　**September 1901 - March 1909**

White House, Washington, DC

Salary: $42,000 USD Per Year
Hours per week: 40

26th President of the United States

In 1904, I won the Presidency by a landslide. "I am no longer a political accident." I introduced new excitement and power to the Presidency by vigorously leading Congress and the American public toward new reforms and a strong foreign policy. As the Steward of the People, I performed the following leadership initiatives, among many others.

KEY LEADERSHIP INITIATIVES:

• Established the Antiquities Act of June 8, 1906. Proclaimed "historic landmarks, historic or prehistoric structures, and other objects of historic or scientific interest" in federal ownership as national monuments. Established conservation actions that helped to impact what would one day become the National Park Service (NPS), which was formally established on August 25, 1916.

• Negotiated disputes over Venezuela, the Dominican Republic, and Morocco. Led the negotiations on the adoption of the Drago Doctrine, which prevented the use of force in collecting foreign debts, an issue increasingly important as the U.S. became more involved with other countries.

• Signed legislation that established five national park units: Crater Lake, Oregon; Wind Cave, South Dakota; Sullys Hill, North Dakota (later designated a game preserve); Mesa Verde, Colorado; and Platt, Oklahoma (now part of the Chickasaw National Recreation Area). By the end of 1906, I had proclaimed four national monuments: Devil's Tower, Wyoming; El Morro, New Mexico; Montezuma Castle, Arizona; and the Petrified Forest, Arizona. I also protected a large portion of the Grand Canyon as a national monument in 1908. During my presidency, I signed into law a total of 18 national monuments.

• In 1905, formed the United States Forestry Service and appointed Gifford Pinchot as the first chief of this new agency. For the first time, lands were reserved for public use and huge irrigation projects were started. The forest reserves in the U.S. went from approximately 43 million acres to about 194 million acres.

Creating Your Five-Page SES Federal Resume

By now, you should have completed the following:

- Your top ten list of accomplishments
- Your accomplishments in the CCAR format
- Your traditional format federal executive resume, ECQ essays, and cover letter

With those three pieces, creating your five-page resume will be fairly simple. Even if you have not completed those steps, you should be able to create your five-page resume.

Step 1: Create Short Accomplishment Bullets

Edit your ECQ and TQ narratives (or top ten list of accomplishments if you have not yet written your ECQs) into short, five- to eight-line bullets or paragraphs. If you are not able to use the full CCAR format for an example, then focus on the accomplishment and the result. Try to highlight a challenge, a context, and an action in at least one of your examples in order to demonstrate the full range of your leadership strengths.

> The five-page SES federal resume should be written with one-inch margins and 12-point font. It may need to be copied and pasted into USAJOBS or another federal resume builder, uploaded as a Word document into USAJOBS or Application Manager, or submitted as a Word attachment via e-mail or hard copy package to be mailed. In all cases, it should not exceed the five-page limit.

Step 2: Resume Template

Using the sample five-page resumes from this book as models, create a similar template outline in your word processing program. Prepare the header with your name, address, phone, email, and the announcement number. Set up topical headers throughout the document: Executive Profile, Experience, Education, Training, Awards, Publications, or other specific topics related to your background or the announcement. Alternatively, if you are converting a traditional federal executive resume, save the file with a new name and use the headers and work experience headings.

Step 3: Writing the Work Experience Section

Job Headers: In the Work Experience section, set up the employment blocks in reverse chronological order, starting with your most recent employer and moving back in time. Include the company or agency with city and state, full dates (months and years for start and end dates), hours worked per week, salary, and a supervisor's name and phone number.

Leadership Duties: Include a short overview of your company's mission and scope of services, followed by a brief description of your leadership duties. The leadership duties become the "Context" from the CCAR from your ECQ stories.

Bulleted List of Accomplishments: Following the leadership duties, include a bulleted list of short accomplishment statements from Step 1. Your resume should highlight ALL of the ECQs and TQs required on a job announcement. To help make sure that you cover all of the requisite ECQs and TQs, identify each bullet in your draft as an ECQ or TQ (Leading Change, Leading People, Results Driven, Business Acumen, Building Coalitions, and so forth), and remove the identifier when you perform your final edit.

It is not necessary to include multiple accomplishments under each work description. However, you do want to ensure that all the ECQs and TQs are addressed within the most recent 10 years, maximizing the use of a variety of diverse stories. You may need to shorten education, training, awards, and other sections to provide additional space for the ECQ and TQ accomplishment bullets.

How Your Five-Page SES Federal Resume Will Be Scored

The resume-based application process is considered a screening method, to be used in conjunction with a structured interview. The evaluators will review all background materials including the vacancy announcement, position description, leadership and technical qualification competency definitions, and relevant benchmarks. They will review the resume materials, evaluate the resume, and assign a rating. The evaluators will identify the executive leadership experience considering the complexity of the position or situation, scope and breadth of the results or outcomes, and the time horizon (how the result affects future issues or events).

For a candidate to be qualified in the Top Group/Highly Qualified and recommended for an interview, the evaluators must identify full mastery of the ECQs and TQs.

When writing the resume interwoven with ECQs, remember to avoid generalities and use specifics that describe the complexity, scope and breadth, and time horizon of your story:

> **BEFORE (Does NOT demonstrate full mastery):** *Customer-oriented Agency expert for IT responsible for end-user satisfaction at all levels. Report to the Agency Head concerning all issues related to IT and innovation.*

> **AFTER (Demonstrates full mastery):** *Leadership oversight for IT requirements for six operating Divisions supporting 10 major programs in three countries. Direct and focus the priorities of 900 personnel and administer a $150M budget. Introduced strategy and associated management approach to transform the Agency's legacy systems, expanding information sharing 30%.*

The after example provided enough detail to show "evidence" of executive leadership, and it provided a "picture" of the scope of leadership and management responsibility of the candidate.

Sample Short Accomplishment Bullets for the Five-Page Resume

Below are shortened versions of the ECQ samples found in Chapter 3. See how we shortened the longer versions and highlighted the important aspects of the accomplishment.

Leading Change

The same Leading Change stories from Chapter 3 are shown below edited down to shorter versions as mini-leadership stories, with evidence of the required ECQ leadership competencies identified from OPM, which can be used as bullets within a five-page SES resume-based application.

When short leadership bullets are integrated into the five-page resume, some information under scope of responsibilities/duties will already be addressed in the resume in the job description/duties overview for each position (e.g., oversight leadership as Chief Information Officer [CIO] for Delta's worldwide technology management with 1,900 people and $350M in planned expenditures within the IT Division). Consequently, that information does not need to be included in the mini-leadership story bullets.

Short Leading Change Bullets

Delta Air Lines Turnaround Story (~75 words / 490 characters with spaces)

- Spearheaded the design of a long-term strategy/operational plan that would stretch corporate view to a three-year horizon by addressing short- and long-term planning, effectively forecasting all expenditures, and creating value for stakeholders. Winning approval from executive councils, the new planning process was embraced as a critical element of the Company's planning regimen. Capital spending dropped by 25% allowing for an increase in the capital spending program, reaching $1.5B.

Economic Transformation in Iraq (~125 words / 855 characters)

- Challenged to focus on the strategic objective of improving the Iraqi economy, I faced numerous obstacles to effecting major organizational changes, in an environment of violence and fluidity: making changes to operational focus, creating capacity in the organization to take on increased work, developing common processes, and introducing infrastructure changes across the enterprise. I led the organization's shift in primary focus and completely revamped my organization's role in the region—I began supporting nation building; addressing NATO issues, growing infrastructure, designating economic safe zones, and building trust amongst the Iraqi business people and public. I led my organization in delivering a wider range of services, with much broader impact—at the national level, and transformed a tactical operation into a strategic powerhouse.

Leading People

The same Leading People samples from Chapter 3 are edited down to the shorter versions below as mini-leadership stories, with evidence of the required ECQ leadership competencies identified from OPM, which can be used as bullets within a five-page SES resume-based application. Every effort was made to ensure that the conflict management and diversity competencies were addressed in the shorter versions.

Short Leading People Bullets

Employee Buy-In for Performance Improvement (~ 75 words / 535 characters with spaces)

- To turn around an underperforming team with the lowest customer satisfaction ratings ever, and put a critical program on track, I had to gain employee "buy-in." I designed employee engagement forums to share my vision, and led discussions seeking ideas for change, commitment, and opportunities to promote inclusion. I applied sensitivity in addressing past performance, and addressed conflict early. My leadership resulted in timely completion of projects, tripling of customer satisfaction ratings, and recognition by other managers.

Low Team Morale (~ 100 words / 720 characters with spaces)

- Empowered a diverse HQ staff with low morale; gained trust and energized a very talented management team and their direct-reports to exceed their potential. The management team handled their direct-reports in a very hierarchical, depreciative manner, resulting in many complaints and personnel turbulence. To establish the new leadership team, I scheduled an off-site meeting. I directed that the meeting be prepared and conducted by the new leadership team, who presented their proposals to senior management. This successful meeting institutionalized the new leadership construct and I achieved an enduring transformation to a leadership culture of inclusion, empowerment, and teamwork. The Region showed markedly improved morale and reduced personnel turbulence.

Results Driven

The same Results Driven samples from Chapter 3 are edited down to shorter versions below as mini-leadership stories, with evidence of the required ECQ leadership competencies identified from OPM, which can be used as bullets within a five-page SES resume-based application. Every effort was made to ensure that results were clearly addressed and presented with an organizational, wide-reaching impact.

Short Results Driven Bullets

Created a New Organizational Structure for Agency (~100 words / 685 characters with spaces)

- Initiated an Agency-wide review of the organizational structure of the Agency; designed a politically sensitive strategy and transformed the entire organizational structure resulting in a drastic reduction of EEO complaints (from 11 to one), the elevation of numerous positions to appropriate grade levels, and a future plan for reducing incorrectly classified grade levels. Employees were briefed on the changes to win support. I crafted a communication plan for Congress explaining the new changes. The organizational structure and strategy I proposed was approved by the Agency, the Senate and House Appropriations Committees, and the EEO and HR Divisions, and was implemented.

Created Profitable Operations (~118 words / 739 characters with spaces)

- I turned around a business that had been hemorrhaging cash for the previous two years. Despite the company's purchase of two plants with capacity to fulfill more than 20% of market demand, the business had not been properly developed. Facing a "start-up" situation, I developed a strategy to address the personnel and business issues, aligned the organization behind key business processes focused on the development of the domestic market, and initiated a hiring and sales training program. I had set the conditions for a robust domestic sales and distribution organization. Within six months, the company doubled its sales volume with domestic sales—a company record, and the company showed a profit for the first time in three years.

Business Acumen

The same Business Acumen samples from Chapter 3 are edited down to the shorter versions below as mini-leadership examples, with evidence of the required ECQ leadership competencies identified from OPM, which can be used as bullets within a five-page SES resume-based application. All three prongs of Business Acumen are addressed in these stories: Financial Management, Human Capital Management, and Technology Management.

Short Business Acumen Bullets

Secured Location for National Center (~ 90 words / 640 characters with spaces)

- I championed the planning and construction of a joint-use public-private facility dedicated to simulation and training, public safety, and forensic science for a University-hosted National Center for Forensic Science. Funding was not available for office space or a facility, so I envisioned a state-funded facility on federal land (no-cost lease) in exchange for office space for federal employees. I gained approvals from Congress, State of Florida, University, DOD, DOJ, Navy Facilities and Engineering Command, Research Park authorities, local regulatory bodies, and others; and approval for state appropriations for construction costs.

NSPS (~100 words / 695 characters with spaces)

- I designed human capital strategies to meet organizational mission and goals, and focused a Process Action Team (PAT) in establishing performance and developmental expectations, policy, and procedures to fully implement the National Security Personnel System (NSPS) for the Naval Audit Service (1,200 personnel). The team also developed an automated system designed as a program management tool. I guided my team to successfully meet the due date, and management approved the performance plans, procedures, business rules, and tools. We achieved our strategic objective of effectively and efficiently implementing the NSPS performance-based plan. All 1,200 auditors attended all NSPS training.

Building Coalitions

The same Building Coalitions samples from Chapter 3 are edited down to the shorter versions below as mini-leadership examples, with evidence of the required ECQ leadership competencies identified from OPM, which can be used as bullets within a five-page SES resume-based application. Every effort was made to ensure that results focused on far-reaching coalition building and partnerships for mutual interests.

Short Building Coalitions Bullets

Missile Defense Coalitions (~65 words / 450 characters with spaces)

- I built a solid coalition between the National Reconnaissance Office (NRO) and the Missile Defense Agency, which is expanding to other Intelligence Community (IC) organizations. I drafted and staffed an overarching Memorandum of Agreement (MOA), which was ultimately signed by the Director NRO and Director MDA. That MOA serves as the keystone document for myriad engagements and formal [funded] projects between these two organizations.

Audit Coalition (~140 words / 865 characters with spaces)

- I led two multi-location overseas audits, while reviewing the Department of Army's checks and balances intended to detect, deter, and prevent fraud, waste, and abuse in contracting operations outside the USA. To lead this audit, I had to coordinate and develop relationships with Senior Leadership officials from 12 different DOD and Department of Army organizations worldwide. This audit was conducted in Africa and Bahrain. All 12 DOD and Army disbursing and contracting Command Activities concurred with the 19 audit recommendations and took immediate action to improve the operations. All six Flag Officers recommended to the Auditor General of the Army the establishment of an audit office in Italy to provide audit coverage for the entire Europe, Africa, and Asia regions. Led completion of the audit in 150 days, 49% less time than normal.

> **It is hard to believe that the five-page SES resume must contain the ECQ accomplishments, TQs, your entire career history featuring your last 10 years of leadership expertise, important certifications, and awards—all in five pages!**

Technical Qualifications for the Five-Page Resume

The samples below are shortened versions from TQ samples found in Chapter 4. These bullets can be added to the five-page SES federal resume.

1. Experience in formulating, developing, implementing, and revising policies, strategies, and processes for national security programs related to natural or other disasters and emergency response (~105 words / 810 characters)

- I spearheaded the transformation of the organization's emergency response apparatus from a traditional, locally focused disaster control element, to a nationally oriented emergency management machine. I merged Air Force, state and local emergency response agencies into one powerful emergency management operation, capable of managing multiple events, while effectively coordinating response actions with many internal and external stakeholders. I established an Air Force Incident Management System (AFIMS)-compliant Emergency Operations Center (EOC) 33% ahead of schedule. For actual and follow-on simulated emergency situations, I reduced the response time needed to establish multi-event command and control by approximately 15-30 minutes, a significant improvement in this time-sensitive environment.

2. Experience in developing and implementing organization-wide operations and processes for deployment, security, and oversight of large scale technology services, and leading broad cultural change in information technology management roles (~130 words / 905 characters)

- Designed the strategy and executed the Law Enforcement Information Sharing Program (LEISP) focused on changing the culture of law enforcement information sharing from "need to know" to "need to share," to systematically improve the investigation and prosecution of criminal activity. Persuaded numerous Agency law enforcement components to support the LEISP. Focused the reallocation of resources to design a data distribution facility to support the publishing and distribution of 100 million records. I guided the dramatic expansion of shareable law enforcement data from 22 million records to 60 million records, and an increase in state and local partnerships from six to more than 32, enabling 2,900 federal, state, local, and tribal law enforcement agencies to enter into productive nationwide information sharing partnerships across the broader federal law enforcement and intelligence community.

3. Experience in developing and implementing organization-wide operations and processes for advanced engineering and manufacturing operations and addressing specific needs or challenges (~70 words / 500 characters)

- I championed and led an Enterprise Resource Planning (ERP) upgrade to meet Sarbanes-Oxley compliance for the corporation and transformed three separate operational structures into one, joining the corporation under one Product Engineering (R&D) Division. All departments adopted and implemented the newly written policies and procedures. During an inspection, only three months after implementation, the entire corporation met and exceeded inspection requirements—a first ever for the corporation.

Case Study 2 – Audit Director (Keith Smith)

Target Agency and Position: Executive Director, Auditing Services, Defense Contract Audit Agency

Keith Smith (name fictionalized) worked with the Department of Defense (in two different agencies) as an auditor for 20 years, successfully moving up the federal ladder reaching the GS-15 level, and was often tapped to serve in an acting Director role for major audits. During his career, he led highly complex audits that saved the DOD up to $900 million. With specialized experience in leading multi-billion dollar audits across the globe, he is also the recipient of major and notable awards.

We developed a top ten list of accomplishments, drafted full CCAR ECQ essays, and then prepared the five-page SES federal resume using short accomplishment bullets (summarized from the longer CCAR ECQ essays). We illustrated his expertise by focusing on the position duties, the technical qualifications, and the 28 SES leadership competencies required for the position. The full package also included an executive cover letter depicting his interest in the position and an overview of his qualifications as a good fit for the position.

The SES resume that we wrote demonstrated that he met the leadership competencies to be referred, interviewed, and selected for an SES position in the agency he targeted; and his ECQs passed the Qualifications Review Board. The final resume includes the keywords identified in bold:

- Knowledge of applicable **laws** and **auditing standards**
- Ability to **manage large auditing or accounting programs** and **organizational elements** with strong emphasis on **policy development**
- Superior knowledge of **advanced fraud auditing techniques**
- Ability to **lead efficient planning and execution** of the **financial management audit program**
- **Delegate** responsibility and authority for program execution to **key staff** and **monitor accomplishment**
- **Collaborate** with the **most senior level military and government** officials to discuss risks and audit progress. Ability to **develop and lead high level working groups**
- **Public speaking**

KEITH SMITH

6916 Thunder Hill Street   202.654.5555
Columbia, MD 20853   keithsmith@gmail.com
Announcement Number: SES-1010 / Executive Director, Auditing Services

---

PROFESSIONAL EXPERIENCE

DEPARTMENT OF DEFENSE, 1995 - PRESENT

Audit Director (YC-3 GS-0511 / GS-15 equivalent), 11/2013 - Present
Department of Army, Washington, DC

- Oversee the activities of 1,000 professional auditors, to include Defense Contract Management Agency, Army Systems Command Earned Value Management Technical Experts, and Defense Contract Agency Audit auditors, divided among five audit teams.
- Supervise a direct-report leadership staff.
- Pointed the way for major financial management control changes to the program and financial management reviews of all DoD major acquisition programs.
- Report directly to the Assistant Auditor General of the Army for Research, Development, and Acquisition Audits.

Supervisory Auditor (GS-0511-15), 09/2005 - 11/2013
Department of Army, Washington, DC

- Responsible for 39 Audit Service auditors to include Systems Command Earned Value Management Technical Experts and Defense Contract Agency Audit Auditors conducting 3,000 audits annually.
- Supervised my staff's planning and simultaneous execution of single and multi-location audit projects involving multimillion-dollar DoD weapon systems acquisition programs geographically dispersed worldwide.
- Briefed and interacted with senior leaders.
- Drafted and established office policy and the staffing structure needed to accomplish the assigned audits.

Program Executive Auditor Advisor, 05/2000 - 09/2005

- Competitively selected to serve as Program Executive Officer (PEO) Auditor to two different Acquisition Commands.
- Program Executive Officer for Air Antisubmarine, Assault, and Special Mission Programs Office; and Air Systems Command, to re-engineer the acquisition auditing process.
- Ensured continuous real-time acquisition auditing, management, and leadership guidance to 42 major program offices executing 300 acquisition programs to nail down achievement of program cost, schedule, and performance objectives.
- Responsible for over 100 modifications and upgrades involving the 300 acquisition programs.

Team Leader, Supervisory Auditor, GS-511-13, 1995 - 2000

- Managed the full range of audit responsibilities for complex areas of weapon systems acquisition and operational audits in the Capitol Region.

EDUCATION

- MBA, University of Maryland
- BS in Accounting, University of Maryland
- Defense Leadership and Management Program (DLAMP), DOD, Washington, DC
- Senior Executive Service Developmental Training, USDA Graduate School
- The Federal Executive Institute, Leadership for Democratic Society
- Defense Acquisition University, Department of Defense Acquisition Program Management Office Course
- Department of the Army Civilian Financial Management Career Program

CERTIFICATIONS

Certified Acquisition Auditor Level III
Defense Acquisition Workforce Improvement Act Level I, Program Management
Contracting Officer Representative

SPEAKING & PUBLICATIONS

Speaker, Defense Audit Agency Training Conference addressing the series of Earned Value Management audits within the Department of Army and Department of Defense

Speaker at the first annual United States Africa Command Contracting Workshop

Co-Author, "Earned Value Management, Is It Working?" The Management Control Program Herald, an Assistant Secretary of the Army for Financial Management Publication

PERFORMANCE AWARDS

Society of Military Comptroller's Meritorious Performance Award for Auditing
Special Act Award
Auditor of the Year

To organize Keith's accomplishments, we developed his top ten list of accomplishments within the past ten years and included a short detail or result for each accomplishment:

1. **Acting Assistant Auditor General**

   Routinely appointed as the Acting Assistant Auditor General for Research, Development, Acquisition, and Logistics Directorate, a Senior Executive Service (SES) level position, with executive management for 60 professional auditors. Brief the Secretary of the Army; the Under Secretary of the Army; the Assistant Secretary of the Army for Research, Development and Acquisition; the Assistant Secretary of the Army for Financial Management and Comptroller; and numerous Flag Officers, Secretariat-level, and other Senior Executives.

2. **Transformed Earned Value Management in DOD**

   Transformed use of Earned Value Management (EVM) within DOD and Department of Army (DA). Led audit to determine what changes were needed to reinvigorate the EVM program and use it effectively across all DOD acquisition programs to achieve its strategic goal of providing affordable weapon systems to Sailors and Marines. The result was use of EVM in DOD and with DOD contractors, ensuring program offices properly used EVM as a management tool and Soldiers and Sailors received affordable, timely weapon systems.

3. **Developed new DOD-wide policies to support launch of Joint Training Program for Defense Acquisition Contractor University**

   Developed and implemented new DOD-wide policies and formed a new DOD working group composed of senior members from all DOD agencies to ascertain priority and proper use of EVM, establish and launch a joint training program at the Defense Acquisition Contractor University, and create a DOD EVM Center to retrain the workforce and implement the policies to control costs for weapons development.

4. **Trained 600 auditors and eliminated time for training**

   Introduced a training program for 600 auditors within the Audit Service to eliminate the time that program personnel spent educating auditors, to dismantle barriers, and to cultivate better relationships between the internal audit and acquisition communities. This program resulted in enhancing the Audit Service's credibility within the acquisition communities, increased our client focus and responsiveness, and expanded our inventory of products and services to meet client needs.

5. **Guided two major overseas audits – Africa and Bahrain**

   Guided the planning and execution of two overseas audits, while reviewing the Department of Army's checks and balances intended to detect, deter, and prevent fraud, waste, and abuse in contracting operations outside the USA. Received full approval for establishment of an audit office in Italy. Led completion of the audit in an accelerated 150 days.

6. **Reengineered acquisition audit process at six major Army Acquisition Commands**

   Spearheaded a reengineering effort of the acquisition auditing process at six major Army Acquisition Commands. My efforts resulted in the acquisition reform initiative changing how the DA Acquisition community views the Army Audit Service. This acquisition reform initiative moved the Program Executive Office to the forefront of implementation of innovative programs.

7. **Published three important audit reports**

   Published three audit reports with full agreement with the audit findings and recommendations resulting in:

   a. DOD organizational changes related to financial management infrastructure, accountability for assets and operations, the reliability of financial information and compliance with public law, acquisition regulations; and

   b. DOD terminating acquisition programs resulting in cost avoidance of $400 million and revising the Army acquisition policy regarding the financial management and oversight for acquisition programs.

8. **Improved morale, reduced conflict and increased productivity of audit team**

   Reversed internal conflict, poor morale and low productivity of an audit team, requested to conduct a politically sensitive audit for the Criminal Investigative Service, with DOD-wide implications. Introduced training and audit execution strategies, and refocused the audit on addressing the potential fraud issues.

9. **Led congressional audit of schedule slippage and contractor cost overruns**

   Led a high-visibility audit of an acquisition program that had experienced significant cost growth and schedule slippage, prompting intense Congressional scrutiny and oversight. Produced two high-impact and quick-reaction audit reports, six months ahead of schedule.

10. **Professional speaking**

   Speaker, Defense Audit Agency Training Conference, addressing the series of Earned Value Management audits within the Department of Army and Department of Defense; Speaker at the first annual United States Africa Command Contracting Workshop.

We expanded Keith's top ten accomplishments into short CCAR stories and identified each story with an appropriate ECQ for use in the five-page SES resume. For this example, we are only setting up five CCAR stories:

1. **Acting Assistant Auditor General** (Leading People / TQ)

   Challenge: I led strategic planning and execution of difficult and complex audits of multimillion-dollar Department of Army (DA) geographically dispersed weapon systems acquisition programs, navigating challenging agency and contractor resistance.

   Context: As the Audit Director, with oversight leadership for 1,000 professional auditors, I was routinely appointed as the Acting Assistant Auditor General for Research, Development, Acquisition, and Logistics Directorate, a Senior Executive Service (SES) level position, with executive management for 60 professional auditors divided among five audit teams.

   Action: I briefed the Secretary of the Army and numerous Flag Officers, Secretariat-level, and other Senior Executives on financial management issues concerning major defense acquisition programs.

   Result: Led my staff in producing numerous organizational improvements, resulting in the establishment of an Earned Value Management (EVM) Integrated Process Team, EVM Center of Excellence, and EVM policy and procedures changes.

2. **Transformed Earned Value Management in DOD** (Leading Change)

   Challenge: I faced furious opposition from the Government and contractor personnel regarding required changes for EVM.

   Context: Led a highly complex audit, requested by the Assistant Secretary of the Army.

   Action: Determined what changes were needed to reinvigorate the EVM program and use it effectively across all DOD acquisition programs to achieve its strategic goal of providing affordable weapon systems to Sailors and Marines.

   Result: Transformed use of Earned Value Management (EVM) within DOD and Department of Army (DA). The results of my change initiative transformed use of EVM in DOD and with DOD contractors, ensuring that program offices properly used EVM as a management tool, and that Soldiers and Sailors received affordable, timely weapon systems.

3. **Developed new DOD-wide policies to support launch of Joint Training Program for Defense Acquisition Contractor University** (Leading Change)

   Challenge: Developed a vision that required buy-in from many stakeholders.

   Context: Developed and implemented new DOD-wide policies.

   Action: Formed a new DOD working group composed of senior members from all DOD agencies to ascertain priority and proper use of EVM.

Result: Established and launched a joint training program at the Defense Acquisition Contractor University, and created a DOD EVM Center to retrain the workforce and implement the policies to control costs for weapons development.

4. **Trained 600 auditors and eliminated time for training** (Business Acumen)

Challenge: Needed to overcome the time that program personnel spent educating auditors, dismantle barriers, and cultivate better relationships between the internal audit and acquisition communities.

Context: Used education and introduced a training program for 600 auditors within the Audit Service.

Action: Developed a strategy to fully integrate myself as a member of the staff to execute this training program. Met with and shared my vision with the two Senior officials; met with their respective Program Managers.

Result: The auditing reform and additional training initiative enhanced the Audit Service's credibility within the acquisition communities, increased our client focus and responsiveness, and expanded our inventory of products and services to meet client needs; 90% of our acquisition audits are now addressing the Army's high risks area.

5. **Guided two major overseas audits: Africa and Bahrain** (Building Coalitions)

Challenge: Guided the planning and execution of two complex multi-location overseas audits, while reviewing the Department of Army's checks and balances intended to detect, deter, and prevent fraud, waste, and abuse in contracting operations outside the USA. There were serious conflicts among the groups as to what the report should address and the direction of recommendations.

Context: As the Audit Director, I led an audit to coordinate and develop relationships with Senior Leadership officials from 12 different Department of Defense and Department of Army Commands and Activities worldwide.

Action: Established a working group/coalition with the 12 DOD activities, and from this working group made recommendations.

Result: All six Flag Officers recommended to the Auditor General of the Army the establishment of an audit office in Italy to provide audit coverage for the entire Europe, Africa, and Asia regions. I led completion of the audit in an accelerated 150 days, 49% less time than normal.

After developing the CCAR essays, we then drafted the resume using the five-page resume-based format and pulled the story bullets into the resume, ensuring that all ECQs, TQs, keywords, and other skills and competencies were addressed in the resume. ECQs are identified here in the sample for your convenience, but the labels would be removed before submission.

KEITH SMITH

6916 Thunder Hill Street   202.654.5555
Columbia, MD 20853   keithsmith@gmail.com

Citizenship: U.S. Citizen
Highest Federal Grade: GS-15
Announcement Number: SES-1010 / Executive Director, Auditing Services

EXECUTIVE PROFILE

Proactive senior leader with proven record of accomplishments leading internal audits across the Department of Defense (DOD) and with the Office of Inspector General, delivering cost effective audits to strengthen federal Agencies and the DOD. Navigate and develop the annual audit plans, and submit audit topics addressing high-risk areas throughout large federal Agencies. Create vision and focus for the development of clear and concise audit objectives and first-ever audit programs for complex areas that lead to identifying significant audit findings.

Broad, deep strategic knowledge of Department of Defense military service specific programs spanning many functional areas including Research and Development, program and budget, support services, financial management, major systems acquisition, supply operations, contracting, and foreign military sales programs. Recommended Department of Defense-wide and federal Agency-wide policy and program changes resulting in cost avoidance and savings of $900 million. Recognized for operational excellence; recipient of the Society of Military Comptroller's Meritorious Award for Auditing, for identifying $400 million in monetary benefits to the Department of Army.

PROFESSIONAL EXPERIENCE & SELECT ACCOMPLISHMENTS

DEPARTMENT OF DEFENSE, 1991 - PRESENT

Audit Director (YC-3 GS-0511 / GS-15 equivalent)   11/2012 - Present
Department of Army, Washington, DC   Hours: 40/Week
Supervisor: Sherri Jones; 555.202.3861 (may be contacted)

Oversee the activities of 1,000 professional auditors, to include Defense Contract Management Agency, Army Systems Command Earned Value Management Technical Experts, and Defense Contract Agency Audit auditors, divided among five audit teams; supervise a direct-report leadership staff. Pointed the way for major financial management control changes to the program and financial management reviews of all DOD major acquisition programs. Report directly to the Assistant Auditor General of the Army for Research, Development, and Acquisition Audits.

- Oversee strategic planning and execution of difficult and complex audits of multimillion-dollar Department of Army (DA) geographically dispersed weapon systems acquisition programs. Navigated through challenging agency and contractor resistance, and drove numerous organizational improvements, resulting in the establishment of an Earned Value Management (EVM) Integrated Process Team, EVM Center of Excellence, and EVM policy and procedures changes within the Department of the Army.

Leadership Accomplishments

- Routinely appointed as the Acting Assistant Auditor General for Research, Development, Acquisition, and Logistics Directorate, with executive management for 60 professional auditors. Brief the Secretary of the Army; Assistant Secretary of Army for Research, Development and Acquisition; the Assistant Secretary of the Army for Financial Management and Comptroller; and numerous Flag Officers, and other Senior Executives on financial management issues concerning major defense acquisition programs.

- Transformed use of Earned Value Management (EVM) within DOD and Department of Army (DA). Led a highly complex audit, requested by the Assistant Secretary of the Army, to determine what changes were needed to reinvigorate the EVM program and use it effectively across all DOD acquisition programs to achieve its strategic goal of providing affordable weapon systems to Sailors and Marines. Crafted an audit strategy plan, and introduced a major shift in the method of conducting business with defense contractors. Led my teams into the offices of major defense contractors to evaluate the adequacy of their EVM systems against industry and DOD standards, a first-ever for the Army Audit Service. Transformed use of EVM in DOD and with DOD contractors; Soldiers and Sailors received affordable, timely weapon systems.

- Spurred the development and implementation of new DOD-wide policies and formed a new DOD working group comprised of senior members from all DOD agencies to ascertain priority and proper use of EVM, establish and launch a Joint training program at the Defense Acquisition Contractor University, and create a DOD EVM Center to retrain the workforce and implement the policies to control costs for weapons development.

- Exploited education and introduced a training program for 600 auditors within the Audit Service to eliminate the time that program personnel spent educating auditors, to dismantle barriers, and cultivate better relationships between the internal audit and acquisition communities. Ninety percent of our acquisition audits are now addressing the Army's high risks area.

- Guided the planning and execution of two complex multi-location overseas audits, while reviewing the Department of Army's checks and balances intended to detect, deter, and prevent fraud, waste, and abuse in contracting operations outside the USA. Formed working relationships with Senior Leadership officials from 12 different DOD and Department of Army organizations worldwide. All 12 DOD and Army disbursing and contracting Command Activities concurred with the 19 audit recommendations. All six Flag Officers recommended to the Auditor General of the Army the establishment of an audit office in Italy to provide audit coverage for the entire Europe, Africa, and Asia regions. I led completion of the audit in an accelerated 150 days, 49% less time than normal.

- Published and edited 12 audit reports with full agreement with the audit findings and recommendations resulting in DOD and DA organizational changes related to financial management infrastructure, accountability for assets and operations, and the reliability of financial information; and development of DA acquisition policy regarding the financial management and oversight for acquisition programs.

SUPERVISORY AUDITOR (GS-0511-15)   **09/2008 - 11/2012**
Department of Army, Washington, DC   **Hours: 40/Week**
Supervisor: John Jones; 202.555.5039 (may be contacted)

Oversaw the work of 39 Audit Service auditors to include Systems Command Earned Value Management Technical Experts and Defense Contract Agency Audit Auditors (GS-14/13/12) conducting 3,000 audits annually valued at $6.4 billion. Provided overarching management and leadership for my staff's planning and simultaneous execution of single and multi-location audit projects involving multimillion-dollar DOD weapon systems acquisition programs geographically dispersed worldwide. Briefed and interacted with senior Department of Army leaders to include Senior Executives and Flag Officers. Drafted and established office policy and the staffing structure needed to accomplish the assigned audits.

Leadership Accomplishments

- Spearheaded a reengineering effort of the acquisition auditing process at six major Army Acquisition Commands within the Department of the Army (DA). Providing oversight guidance to 26 major program offices executing 119 acquisition programs, I ensured achievement of program cost, schedule, and performance objectives. Crafted an audit strategy to execute this reform initiative and shared my vision with the six Senior Acquisition officials and their respective Program Managers. My efforts resulted in the acquisition reform initiative changing how the DA Acquisition community views the Army Audit Service. This acquisition reform initiative moved the Program Executive Office to the forefront of implementation of innovative programs.

- Published three audit reports with full agreement with the audit findings and recommendations resulting in:

  - DOD organizational changes related to financial management infrastructure, accountability for assets and operations, the reliability of financial information and compliance with public law, acquisition regulations; and

  - DOD terminating acquisition programs resulting in cost avoidance of $400 million and revising the Army acquisition policy regarding the financial management and oversight for acquisition programs. Briefed the Secretary of Army on the results of the audit of Non-Acquisition Programs identifying $400 million in cost savings to the Department of Army.

- Reversed internal conflict, poor morale and low productivity of an audit team, requested to conduct a politically sensitive audit for the Criminal Investigative Service, with DOD-wide implications. I took charge of the audit team, introduced training and audit execution strategies, and refocused the audit on addressing the potential fraud issues. These efforts greatly improved the team's level of expertise of specialized auditing functions, allowing the team to be responsive to leadership in managing a high-risk area by providing audit services of recognizable value. The audit team identified a security vulnerability involving contractor employees accessing restricted and controlled areas on Air Force, Army, Navy, and Marine Corps installations across the U.S. The report went to Chief of Army Operation Security Office and OSD Security Office.

- Led a high-visibility audit of an acquisition program that had experienced significant cost growth and schedule slippage, prompting intense Congressional scrutiny and oversight. Mentored and coached the new program manager and exposed the team to the requirements of the acquisition program by introducing advanced formal training. I obtained technical support from Subject Matter Technical Experts, to support our review of the contractors' accounting and management systems. Under my guidance, this audit team produced two high-impact and quick-reaction audit reports, six months ahead of schedule.

Program Executive Auditor Advisor   **05/2004 - 09/2008**
Grade / Salary: GS-511-14. Hours: 40/Week
Supervisor: Tom Linder; 555.210.4509 (may be contacted)

Competitively selected as Program Executive Officer (PEO) Auditor to two different Acquisition Commands—Air Antisubmarine, Assault, and Special Mission Programs Office; and Air Systems Command—to re-engineer the acquisition auditing process. Ensured continuous real-time acquisition auditing, management, and leadership guidance to 42 major program offices executing 300 acquisition programs to nail down achievement of program cost, schedule, and performance objectives. Guided more than 100 modifications and upgrades involving the 300 acquisition programs with annual budget of $5 billion.

Leadership Accomplishments

- Shared acquisition knowledge with 700 other auditors within the Audit Service resulting in the elimination of time program personnel spent educating auditors.

- Dismantled barriers and cultivated better relationships between the internal audit and acquisition communities, enhancing the Audit Service's credibility, increasing our client focus and responsiveness, and expanding our inventory of products and services to meet client needs.

- Received a Letter of Appreciation from the Deputy Commander for Acquisition and Operation, a Senior Executive, for my contributions toward establishing the initial Integrated Program Team (IPT) Training Course.

Team Leader, Supervisory Auditor, GS-511-13, 2001 - 2004

- Managed the full range of audit responsibilities for complex areas of weapon systems acquisition and operational audits in the Capitol Region.

EDUCATION

- **MBA,** University of Maryland, 2005
- **BS in Accounting,** University of Maryland, 1994
- **Defense Leadership and Management Program** (DLAMP), DOD, Washington, DC, 2014
- **Senior Executive Service Developmental Training,** USDA Graduate School, 2012
- **The Federal Executive Institute,** Leadership for Democratic Society, 2011
- **Defense Acquisition University,** Department of Defense Acquisition Program Management Office Course, 2006
- **Department of the Army Civilian Financial Management Career Program,** 2003

DEFENSE ACQUISITION RELATED CERTIFICATIONS

- Certified Acquisition Auditor Level III
- Defense Acquisition Workforce Improvement Act Level I, Program Management
- Contracting Officer Representative

PROFESSIONAL SPEAKING ENGAGEMENTS & PUBLICATIONS

- Speaker, Defense Audit Agency Training Conference addressing the series of Earned Value Management audits within the Department of Army and Department of Defense, 2015
- Speaker at the first annual United States Africa Command Contracting Workshop, 2014
- Co-Author, "Earned Value Management, Is it Working?" The Management Control Program Herald, an Assistant Secretary of the Army for Financial Management Publication, 2013

PERFORMANCE AWARDS

- Society of Military Comptroller's Meritorious Performance Award for Auditing
- Special Act Award
- Auditor of the Year

The Executive Cover Letter is not included with this case study,
because a cover letter would count toward your five page limit.

See the rest of Judy Johnson's case study, including the background, before resume, Executive Federal Resume, USAJOBS resume, ECQs, and cover letter in Chapter 6 starting on page 78.

JUDY JOHNSON

Permanent:
5420 Constantine Avenue • Washington, DC 92865

Judy@gmail.com
Cell: 555.202.4986

Citizenship: U.S. | Military Status: Active Duty U.S. Army
Announcement Number: SES-20XX, Executive Director, Mobilization & Training, Dept. of Navy

EXECUTIVE PROFILE

Major General, U.S. Army (Active & Reserve), 20-year career
15-year Corporate Career / Senior Sales and Marketing Executive
Multi-lingual: German & French | TS/SCI

Senior executive with full oversight direction for strategic planning and business leadership for large, geographically separated organizations, hundreds of employees and multi-million dollar operating budgets, while holding dual careers with multi-national, fast-moving consumer goods corporations, and in leading U.S. Army organizations. Develop policy and regulatory compliance. Culturally acclimatized, politically correct, and diplomatic; excellent political-military skills. Structure joint operations.

• • •

U.S. Army (Active & Reserve Components) Experience, 1995 - Present

Major General, U.S. Army Reserve (Active Duty)	**05/2014 - Present**
Deputy Chief of Staff, Washington, DC and Headquarters Europe	**Hours per week: 40**
Supervisor: John Jones; 555.398.3800; Contact: Yes	**Salary: $150K per year**

Principal advisor to Commanding General (Director-equivalent), U.S. Army Europe on all Reserve Component affairs, activities, and policy development. Monitor processes for training and readiness of the Reserve Components to meet security and force protection objectives. Liaison between Commanding General, U.S. Army Europe and Chief, Army Reserve and Director, Army National Guard for development of plans, policies, procedures, and guidance for coordination and synchronization of Reserve Components integration into U.S. Army Europe peacetime training support, as well as contingency operations. Represent leadership at exercises, conferences and other activities involving Reserve Component personnel and issues, to include distinguished visitors to the U.S. Army Europe area of responsibility.

Key Leadership Initiatives:

• Oversaw two major Army and Air Force exercises. Led a multi-service staff and multiple Army and Marine organizations in planning and execution as part of a U.S.-led Joint Task Force operating in a sovereign host nation. Guided senior staff in determining the personnel strength required for both combat and post-combat phases; setting the Theater for port, airfield and basing needs; coordinating flow in and staging of forces and materiel; conducting ground combat operations, synchronizing with Air Force, Navy and Special Operations Forces counterparts; managing immediate post-combat stability and humanitarian relief operations, as well as redeployment of U.S. forces and transition of the land forces mission to the host nation and international organizations. **(Leading People/Results Driven/Business Acumen)**

- As a result of successful performance, appointed Deputy Exercise Director for the next Fiscal Year's major exercise, which entails mentoring an active component major general (senior level) and leading the ground force activities of the Joint Exercise Control Group. **(Leading People)**
- Deputy Chief of Staff, Operations, U.S. Army Europe for several months. Oversight leadership for 1,200 military personnel and civilians and 21 divisions, supporting war plans, training, exercises and international operations for 70,000 Soldiers in U.S. Army Europe; as well as the deployment and redeployment of U.S. Army Europe units and individuals to Iraq and Afghanistan for Operations Enduring Freedom and Iraqi Freedom. **(Results Driven)**
- Exercise Director for U.S. Army Europe Foreign Consequence Management exercises, which test the ability of U.S. Army Europe and U.S. European Command to respond to foreign chemical, biological, radiological and nuclear incidents, in coordination with the U.S. Department of State and host nation ministries of interior and indigenous consequence management forces. **(Building Coalitions)**
- Spearheaded U.S. Army Reserve (USAR) Schools Initiative in U.S. Army Europe, increasing interoperability by teaching U.S. military doctrine to foreign military partners and the U.S. interagency. **(Results Driven)**

Major General, U.S. Army Reserve (Active Duty)   05/2012 - 05/2014
Deputy Director Planning, the Pentagon, Washington, DC   Hours per week: 40
Supervisor: Jerry Winters; 555.497.4488; Contact: Yes   Salary: $150K per year

Advised Director, Strategic Plans in support of Chairman, Joint Chiefs of Staff top calendar issues for defense plans and programs. Served as Host Team Leader for Chemical Weapons Convention Challenge Inspections and annual challenge inspection exercises. Expert at annual NATO Crisis Management exercise. Represented the Organization and top leadership at international conferences, Joint Staff Talks, and other events.

Key Leadership Initiatives:

- Senior U.S. military representative at U.S. Department of State-led conferences and negotiations: Organization for Security and Cooperation in Europe, Proliferation Security Initiative, and EUCOM-sponsored conference for the Economic Union Of West African States. At Proliferation Security Initiative conference, participated in negotiations with Russian contingent to achieve tangible commitments to this critical undertaking. **(Building Coalitions)**
- Conducted diplomatic negotiations gaining respect of allied hosts. Directly contributed to Mexico's decision to begin Joint Staff Talks; led the annual Joint Staff Talks with Chile. **(Building Coalitions)**

Brigadier General, U.S. Army Reserve (Active Duty)   05/2008 - 05/2012
3rd Army Reserve Command, Germany   Hours per week: 40
Supervisor: Andrew K. Myers; 555.202.2002; Contact: Yes   Salary: $150K per year

Led a major subordinate organization of United States Army Europe, composed of 34 units and 2,000 Reserve and Active-duty Soldiers, and civilian employees. Full accountability for ensuring subordinate units were manned, properly trained, and maintained a high rate of readiness for mobilization. Administered, planned, and executed an operating budget of $30M. Recommended and instituted a routine mobilization preparedness regimen, and associated issuing guidance, for all units including enhanced measures in response to 9/11 to ensure personnel and unit mobilization readiness across the organization.

Key Leadership Initiatives:

- Realigned force structure to meet the evolving needs of the total Army. Initiated an annual force structure review process with HQ U.S. Army Europe (USAREUR) and its major subordinate commands. **(Leading Change)**

- Guided implementation of Equipment Storage Site-Expanded concept, producing a validated 97% equipment serviceability rate from previous 75%, in just one year. Outsourced logistics, increasing by 25% the time for units to focus precious training time on their core competency: mission operations. **(Results Driven)**

- Consolidated units into Reserve Centers, achieving greater return on investment in facilities and automation infrastructure, as well as synergies in administration and training. **(Leading Change/ Results Driven)**

- Conducted negotiations with German Federal defense and finance ministries, gained HQ U.S. Army Europe support, and achieved NATO "member of the force" status for the organization's drilling Reservists, thereby providing them the same PX and commissary access as Reserve Soldiers in the USA. **(Building Coalitions/Results Driven)**

Previous Military Assignments (Reserve Duty)

- 7th U.S. Army Reserve Command, Deputy Chief of Staff Operations, Chief of Staff in HQs. Various command and staff positions at subordinate units, Germany, 1998 to 2008

- Army National Guard, Liaison Officer 42nd Division Artillery, New York, 1995 to 2004

Consumer Goods USA, 15-YEAR INDUSTRY CAREER

Executive Vice President   **05/2006 - 05/2008**
Long Beach, CA   **Hours per week: 40**
Supervisor: Mr. Tom Hansen; 555.349.2940; Contact: Yes   **Salary: $150K per year**

* Consumer Goods USA is an international business with 25,000 employees in 20 countries.

Implemented a strategic vision for business operations and development in the USA region of this international company with offices in 20 countries. Indirectly supervise an office staff of 65 and sales force of 80, with dotted-line supervision to 175 plant workers, and independent distributors across five countries. I manage cross-cultural issues, enforce EEO regulations, and create programs to heighten morale and foster diversity. Manage an operational budget worth $7.9M.

Key Leadership Initiatives:

- Integrated the brands, employees, distributors and business operations of a major company acquisition in 2009. **(Business Acumen)**

- Achieved annual and strategic plan (3-year planning horizon) volume and profit targets. **(Results Driven)**

- Empowered and coached a diverse staff with low morale; gained trust and energized a very talented management team and their direct-reports to exceed their potential. Led a headquarters' staff in Long Beach composed of personnel from two U.S. regions, the Headquarters, and members from two counties. This comprised the management team and the mid-level staff. The management team handled their direct-reports in a very hierarchical, depreciative manner, resulting in many complaints and personnel turbulence. To establish the new leadership team, I scheduled an off-site meeting and directed that the meeting be prepared and conducted by the new leadership team, who presented their proposals to management. This successful meeting institutionalized the new leadership construct and I achieved a leadership culture of inclusion, empowerment, and teamwork. The HQ staff showed markedly improved morale and reduced personnel turbulence. (Leading People)

- Ensured full integration of new plant in Long Beach. Melded marketing and sales organization from east coast for office support (Finance, IT, Logistics, Legal & HR) and ensured cooperation between HQ marketing and sales departments, HQ R&D and Global Supply Chain. (Building Coalitions)

- Developed, agreed upon, and implemented a strategic vision for Consumer Goods USA's business operations across the nation and the plants in 20 other countries to standardize operations reflecting 5- to 10-year assessment of regional trends including Free Trade Agreements; market regulatory trends; trade evolution; and competitive strategies. Incorporated relevant elements into annual and strategic business objectives, plans, programs and budgets, including organizational and business mode shifts. (Leading Change)

Vice President, Corporate Marketing Initiatives   05/2004 - 05/2006
Cincinnati, Ohio   Hours per week: 40
Supervisor: Mr. Donald Anderson: 495.874.9230; Contact: Yes   Salary: $150K per year

Corporate-wide single point of contact for corporate marketing and regulatory compliance and initiatives. Developed and implemented Direct Marketing vision, strategies, programs and budgets. Supervised 100+ staff and administered $47M marketing budget. Articulated Regulatory market instructions for Annual & Strategic Plan HQ instructions.

Key Leadership Initiatives:

- Formed and actively managed the Regulatory Compliance Working Group in creating strategic and contingency plans for corporate response to regulatory trends. Ensured that financial and commercial impacts of directives were incorporated into Headquarters and individual market operating and strategic plans. (Business Acumen)

- Guided development of and achieved the on-time, on-budget implementation of a corporate-wide consumer products directive, which saved the company $45 million over five years. Compliance with the directive was named a corporate priority for the upcoming three-year period, as the out-year's corporate budget planning was already underway, and thus would have visibility with the Board of Directors. (Results Driven)

- Led implementation of corporate-wide Internet-based direct marketing pilot program, which was so successful that is was adopted corporate-wide and expanded to cell phone coverage and social media. (Business Acumen)

Vice President, Imports   05/2002 - 05/2004
Long Beach, CA   Hours per week: 40
Supervisor: Mr. James Smith; 555.349.7811; Contact: Yes   Salary: $150K per year

Reported to Regional President as member of Regional Executive Committee. Supervised senior staff of 28. Managed all aspects of importation of $70M sales of high-margin premium and sub-premium brands from five countries.

Key Leadership Initiatives:

- Successfully disengaged from importers, thwarting importer strategy of multi-million dollar cash extraction and disturbance of commercial operations. **(Business Acumen)**

- Directed multi-functional team of operations in five countries: R&D, HQ packaging, plant, and marketing and sales staff to ensure synchronized product, packaging, operations planning, marketing and selling activities. **(Leading People)**

- Secured return of bank guarantees of $28 million via successful negotiations with foreign customs authorities, as well as rigorous project management of simultaneous product disposal and excise stamp recovery operations in two major cities. **(Business Acumen)**

- Successfully redeployed key managers via intensive personal networking, as well as coaching/ mentoring and exposure via delegating direct responsibility for projects. **(Leading People)**

Earlier Position

General Manager, Consumer Goods USA, 2000 - 2002 (Long Beach, CA)

Complete P&L responsibility for more than $100M in domestic sales, distribution and marketing of products manufactured in two local plants and imported from five countries. Reported to Regional President. Directly supervised 19 director-level staff and office staff of 60 at the HQ office. Oversight direction for 120-strong field sales force and 2,000 plant employees across the USA.

- Turned around a business that had been hemorrhaging cash for previous two years. Rallied organization behind vision statement. Achieved control of imports of high-margin premium brands formerly managed by Export Department. Instituted sales/marketing programs to fully align and motivate staff, sales force and trade behind the newfound Total Brand Portfolio Management. Closed two plants, securing $12M in cost savings. **(Business Acumen)**

EDUCATION & U.S. ARMY PROFESSIONAL MILITARY EDUCATION

- Master of Business Administration, University of Maryland, 2003
- Bachelor of Science in International Relations, University of Virginia, 1993
- National Security Management Course, National Defense University, 2014
- U.S. Army Command and General Staff Officer Course, 2013

PUBLIC SPEAKING ENGAGEMENTS

- "U.S. Army Europe in Transformation." Delivered speech in German, 2015
- American Chamber of Commerce Serbia, and Serbian and international press. "Update on International Operations and Investments in Serbia," Serbia, 2014
- Press conference, UN Palace of Nations, Geneva, Switzerland, 2013

Conferences / Symposia

- Annual Serbia and Albania Economist Intelligence Unit conferences, 2008 - present
- First Annual Proliferation Security Initiative Conference, Warsaw, Poland, 2011

OTHER

Languages: German 3/3 • French 3/3

Military Awards & Decorations: Legion of Merit • Defense Meritorious Service Medal • Meritorious Service Medal • Army Commendation Medal • Army Achievement Medal

Clearance: TS/SCI

Chapter Eight

Lessons Learned

Top Writing Tips for Senior Executives When SES ECQs are Disapproved by Office of Personnel Management's Qualifications Review Board (QRB)

It is startling and a very rude wake-up to receive an OPM Qualifications Review Board disapproval letter on your ECQ narratives. The narratives took many hours to write, and you ARE a true leader and expert for the position.

The OPM QRB emails and comments are stunningly honest and can be disappointing and shocking. However, if you are truly qualified, the problem is not YOU.

It's your ability to write in leadership language, demonstrate your past performance in real proven numbers and action, or perhaps your inability to write about your leadership competencies in the required format. Also, you may have missed the required CCAR format.

So, get over the disappointment, and carefully read the comments in your disapproval letter. Follow the QRB directions completely. Rewrite the narratives that are disapproved and use the CCAR formula. Hopefully, your next submission will be successful!

You may also consider getting expert professional writing and editing help for your re-submission, because you will get one chance to re-submit.

Writing Tip #1: Write effectively and clearly.

Each ECQ should be assessed for relevance, clarity, detail, objectiveness, and effectiveness.

The written documents submitted to an agency and the Qualifications Review Board must persuasively demonstrate decision-making and leadership abilities, indicating evidence of the 28 leadership competencies required of OPM. Write in an active voice at an executive level. Articulate specific examples and avoid use of vague descriptions. Responses should convey actions and clearly describe the difference that your leadership created within an organization.

Spell out acronyms, avoid jargon, and describe ranks and terms that may be misunderstood. A member of the QRB many not be familiar with your functional area of expertise or even your agency/company. Do not assume the readers will understand your position, even when using what might be considered standard acronyms.

Avoid passive construction or bureaucratic phrasing:
- A passive sentence structure may read: Responsible for; tasked with...
- An active sentence structure may read: I decided; I directed; I led...

Avoid generalities or vague references:
- *Vague:* I manage a staff of 18 supporting policy development.
- *Clarify:* I lead an office with 18 senior interagency personnel detailed from six different agencies. Guide staff in policy development and planning to improve the sharing and dissemination of information across the government for national security.

Writing Tip #2: Translate acronyms, jargon, and ranks.

Acronyms: Always spell out acronyms in the first instance. For example, PMA could be an acronym for: President's Management Agenda, Promotion Marketing Association, or Project Management Association. EVP (Executive Vice President) and CIO (Chief Information Officer) may seem commonplace, but they need to be spelled out in the first instance within each document.

Jargon: Jargon is specialized language relating to a specific activity, profession, group, or event. For example, "Commander 9th Army Reserve Command (9th ARCOM)" could be translated to CEO or Executive Officer of an organization based in Europe with 7,000 people in 14 different locations dispersed throughout four countries.

Military Ranks: Be mindful when using military rank or acronyms. For example, a Captain in the Army is a junior officer; a Captain in the Navy is a senior officer. Be sure to describe the appropriate scope of leadership when using military ranks and other terms.

Tip: Use the Readability Statics function in Microsoft Word to determine characters/word lengths, percentage of passive sentences, and the reading grade level.

Lessons learned from disapproval letters:

- Spell out acronyms, even common ones such as CIO.
- Make sure your narratives are not jargon-heavy.
- Do not use "i.e." or "e.g." Instead, use "that is" or "for example," respectively.

Writing Tip #3: Write stories that are relevant and recent; avoid opinions, beliefs, and philosophies.

The government seeks executives who are ready to lead in today's ever-changing environment and who are current with legislation and activities happening in Congress. Use recent examples focusing on the past three to five years, when possible, and expand to no more than ten years. Additionally, the QRB is focused on what you have done as a manager and leader, so your examples need to cover your "hands-on" experience and focus on accomplishments. Use "I" statements, instead of "we" statements, taking full credit for leading organizations to produce results.

Lessons learned from disapproval letters:

- Do not use stories more than 1tenyears old.
- Use "I" statements—take ownership of your accomplishments.
- Change all the "we" entries to "I" entries. Change "We..." to "I led my staff..."
- Remove personal philosophy from your narrative. Avoid "in my opinion."
- Do not include negative comments about a particular group.

Writing Tip #4: Follow the CCAR (Challenge, Context, Action, Result) model.

OPM's recommended format for writing the Executive Core Qualifications is CCAR, to ensure all elements of each story are clear to the reader. The QRB members look for evidence of the CCAR format within the context of the essays and within the five-page resume-based application. It is easy to make laundry lists of duties and accomplishments, but the lists need to be drafted into CCAR essay stories that flow and are easy to read and understand.

Lessons learned from disapproval letters:

- Use ALL of the CCAR components for each story when possible.
- Present a clear picture of the substantive challenges and context rather than a list of duties.
- Make your CCAR components easy to identify.
- Strengthen your results.

Writing Tip #5: Be specific and illustrate results with qualitative and quantitative examples.

Use precise numbers to describe budgets, personnel, dates (timeframe), and other factors. Avoid use of "various," "numerous," or "several"—these are terms that make people guess. Convey enough familiarity with the results, and the methods by which they were achieved, to ensure the reader understands the full context of the environment and the achievement.

As you write your accomplishment and results, make a comparison between the organization/situation before you led change and after you achieved the change.

Lessons learned from disapproval letters:

- Use dollar amounts, percentages, and numbers in your results.
- Make your results as strong and clear as possible.
- Instead of, "Finally..." write, "This resulted in..." This makes the results easy for the reader to identify.
- Write-ups for Leading Change and Leading People are often too narrow in scope. Address changes you made to the entire organization and the impact of those changes on the organization.

Writing Tip #6: Write about leadership.

Your ECQs must demonstrate effective application of what you know as an executive leader. The ECQs should not merely describe personal growth, but rather describe the difference that you made that reached and influenced other people, other organizations, and policies.

Write about major accomplishments, not about how you developed skills. Many of the KSA (knowledge, skills, and abilities) statements written for General Schedule positions are effective when candidates demonstrate progressive responsibility, increasingly complex skill sets, or movement up the career ladder. However, the SES selects candidates who can demonstrate, through their leadership and management accomplishments, that they are capable of leading an organization now.

Review each ECQ to see how your example:
- reflects innovation
- describes your talent
- matches other examples
- amplifies your explanation of the challenges you faced
- presents the specifics of your solutions
- explores what distinguishes you
- uses objective instead of subjective descriptors

Lessons learned from disapproval letters:

Leading Change

- Show evidence of strategic thinking or vision.
- Include specific actions of how you led change.
- Describe the transformation that occurred. Show how it went beyond just an improvement of current processes.
- Demonstrate how you led change at the executive level.
- Write about any changes you caused to happen outside your organization.

Tip: Ask the following questions to help define how you led change:

- Is the organizational vision evident?
- Did I transcend vision into action?
- Is it evident that I strategically initiated and implemented transformational change?

Leading People

- Show how you pulled together a team, motivated them, and personally influenced the outcome despite challenges.
- Talk about instances where you leveraged diversity or managed conflict.
- Give examples of how you created an environment that affords independence and efficient action in order to meet the organization's needs.

Tip: Ask the following questions to help define how you led people:

- What is the largest staff I led; what were the challenges in leading this large staff?
- How did I lead the team through a challenge?
- How did I deal with conflicts that arose within the team?

Results Driven

- Make your results very clear.
- Focus on what the organization accomplished with you in charge.

Tip: Ask the following questions to help define how you delivered results:

- How did the priorities and objectives I set lead to high quality/quantity results?
- How did I address the needs of stakeholders and customers (internal and external)?
- How did I identify problems and implement solutions that resulted in improved services?

Business Acumen

- Include solid evidence of actual financial and human capital management.
- Discuss your human capital management experience (defined as building and managing workforces based on organizational goals, budget considerations, and staffing needs;

ensuring employees are appropriately recruited, selected, appraised, and rewarded; taking actions to address performance problems). Don't blend with Leading People competencies.

- Technology management should include online and multi-media staff training and use of social media.

Tip: Ask the following questions to help define how you demonstrated business acumen:

- What is my experience in creating and administering budgets and resources? Is it evident?

- What is my experience with a multi-sector workforce? What percentage of backlog was eliminated or reduced?

- How did I utilize technology to create or improve programs? What difficulties did I address in integrating this technology?

Building Coalitions

- Explain how you brought groups together or developed relationships between two or more organizations.

- Demonstrate that you not only organized groups, but led them as well.

Tip: Ask the following questions to help define how you built coalitions:

- What groups/networks (internal and external) did I partner with to achieve goals?

- How did I bring groups together? What challenges did I face?

- How did I build alliances and gain help and support to accomplish organizational goals?

Writing Tip #7: Cite recent education and training.

Include continual education that enhances skills in particular factors (for example, to address the cross-cutting fundamental leadership competency: "Continual Learning"). If education or training is included, it needs to be specific, executive level, and recent (training completed within the past five years is considered recent).

Here are some examples of recent, targeted education and advanced professional development:

- Graduate of the Reid Buckley School of Public Speaking and the Karrass Seminar for Effective Negotiating

- Master of Arts/Strategic Communication and Leadership, Seton Hall University

- Defense Information School Public Affairs Officer Qualification Course, Advanced Distributed Learning, Resident (12 months)

- Senior Executive Service Developmental Training, USDA Graduate School, Washington, DC

Writing Tip #8: Proofread and edit all written documents.

Believe it or not, the QRB will actually point out your typos in a disapproval letter. Draftsmanship and executive writing are critical to a well-prepared SES application package. Executive writing includes understanding your audience and the purpose of the documents; writing effectively, clearly, and concisely; using active voice; using leadership terms (for example, instead of, "I assisted the agency head," write, "I advised the agency head"); and developing stories that are persuasive with a strategic message that delivers results. What you say matters to the readers; impart a compelling message and the strength of your leadership qualifications. OPM is expecting a professional and polished document. Proofread and edit all written documents more than once and ask a friend, family member, or colleague to also proofread your written documents. Print out your document and proof on paper, not just on the computer. If time affords, let your document sit for a day before you proof. Read it aloud to check flow.

Use spell check, but do not reply on it*. For example, "manger" is a perfectly good word that will not be flagged as a misspelling in the spell check function, and without a thorough proofreading, "manger" may replace "manager" in the document.

Tip: Draft all written documents in a Word file, and then copy and paste or transfer the information to online builders. Do not draft resumes and ECQs in online builders, as you have greater opportunity to make typographical and grammatical errors, and, in some cases, you may not be able to retrieve what you wrote. You always want to keep a record of your submission.

Lessons learned from disapproval letters:

- Avoid typos like "contacting resources" (should be "contracting resources") that spell check will not catch.

- Check for missing words, such as "neglected the opportunity [to] improve operations".

- Make sure what you wrote makes sense.

Writing Tip #9: Follow the "How to Apply" instructions perfectly.

Analyze the submission requirements carefully to ensure that you are submitting the required documentation, which may be a five-page resume-based application, or an executive federal resume and set of ECQs and TQs (the announcement may specify if the narratives can be one or two pages or a certain character length). Some announcements also request copies of transcripts, an SF-50 (federal personnel action), references, writing samples, or other requirements. Candidates may be disqualified for not submitting a complete package.

* Note: The error in this sentence is a perfect example to demonstrate the point being made.

Consider Professional Assistance with Your SES Application

The Resume Place has had a 100% success rate with rewriting disapproved SES applications! You only get one opportunity to resubmit your package, so it may be worthwhile to consider getting expert insight and assistance. Here are a few of our satisfied customers:

"I am so thankful to you for rewriting my ECQs after I was disapproved from OPM. I was surprised that I was disapproved, and very discouraged. So, your work and expertise in rewriting my ECQs were a blessing! Thank you for your hard work and technical guidance in helping me tell my leadership stories and meet the leadership competencies for each ECQ. I was approved on the second round."

"I can't tell you how much I appreciate the work you did to make me look good! Without your efforts my paperwork would not have been approved. I owe it all to you." – *U.S. Secret Service, Special Agent, approved on rewrite*

"Wanted you to know I got certified by OPM Friday. I report in two weeks. Thanks for all your efforts on my behalf." – *HUD OIG, Special Agent in Charge, approved on rewrite*

"Thank you for your guidance in helping me through a re-write of ECQs 2 and 3. I was notified yesterday that the OPM QRB approved my appointment into an SES position in DHS."

"I just wanted to let you know that I just found out that my ECQs were approved!!!! Thank you so very much!!!!" – *USDOT OIG candidate*

"Thank you again for your help with my SES package. The process was long and drawn-out, but it was all worth it, because I got one of the two jobs I applied for! The package you helped me with must have been pretty good, because I was never asked to make any edits. I could not imagine having started the SES/ECQ package in Nov. when it was first advertised... I'll be telling everyone to have draft ECQs and MTQs ready and up-to-date for when they see a job they are interested in."

"I just found out my ECQs just passed QRB, so you are still batting 100% pass rate!! Thank you." – *Dept. of Commerce SES candidate, approved on rewrite*

"I just got notification today that I've been officially accepted into the 2013-14 Asian American Government Executives Network SES Candidate Development Program! Your assistance and expertise with my résumé and ECQs were absolutely the difference makers in this process. I am speechless and want to express my sincerest 'THANK YOU!!!!' for your help."

"Thank you, thank you, thank you for your guidance, professionalism, patience, and expertise. I am certain that my success was due in large part to you! I've recommended the services of the Resume Place to several SES hopefuls, and have encouraged them to use you from the very beginning. Working with you was indeed a joy, and worth every single penny! Did I say thank you?? THANK YOU!!!!"

"I want to thank you for all of your support, direction, counsel, and advice during the ECQ development phase of our time together. The ECQ package that your crafted sailed through the QRB, and I was approved for the SES position. I could not have done it without you."

"I wanted to share my good news with you! Finally after 6+ months, I was notified that I got the SES job. I have your assist to thank for my big turnaround from my first SES interview to the next. The feedback from the selecting official was I improved my performance 200%! So thanks again for your assist in writing skills, interview techniques, and a change in my perspective about what I do for a living. What a confidence builder you are for anyone who has the opportunity to use your professional services."

Chapter Nine

The Structured Interview and the ECQ Grid

SAMPLE SES ANNOUNCEMENT WITH KEYWORDS IN BOLD

Job Title: Director, Weapons and Materials Research Directorate
Department: Department of the Army
Agency: U.S. Army Research, Development and Engineering Command

While assigned to the U.S. Army Research Laboratory (ARL), U.S. Army Research, Development and Engineering Command (RDECOM), U.S. Army Materiel Command (AMC), the Director, Weapons and Materials have a substantial impact on U.S. and allied national defense efforts and the design and selection of material and equipment. This position is responsible for **total directorate mission** which involves **all aspects of ballistics research**; weapons & armaments technologies; armor & survivability and materials and manufacturing research & technologies. Responsibility includes establishing and maintaining strong and viable weapons systems-oriented basic research programs in physics, chemistry, mathematics and engineering related to long-term Army needs and directed toward **overcoming technological barriers and obtaining solutions to technological problems** in defense-related weapons systems survivability and lethality technologies. Incumbent serves as the **RDECOM Technology Focus Team leader** for **investment portfolio recommendations** across the command in the areas of Ballistics, materials, protection and lethality technologies; focuses work on the U.S. Army Training and Doctrine Command (TRADOC) requirements and recommends programs and investment strategy across the command to meet these war fighter needs . The **Director leads a workforce of approximately 450 civilian** professional, scientific, administrative, technical, military and support personnel using a broad knowledge of physical sciences and associated engineering and mathematics.

The Structured Interview

A structured interview is one in which all candidates are asked the same questions by an interview panel, in the same order, and in more or less the same way. Of course, interviews have long been an essential method for deciding whether a candidate is a "good fit" for a given position. But the structured interview takes this technique to the next level by giving each applicant an equal chance to respond and then scoring those responses systematically so that candidates can be compared objectively.

Structured interviews are becoming an important part of the SES application process for a couple of reasons. First, OPM requires agencies to perform structured interviews based on the Executive Core Qualifications when using the resume-based selection process described above. In the absence of the usual narrative statements addressing the ECQs, agencies would otherwise not have enough information to make a valid selection. In effect, the interview fills the gap left by missing ECQ statements by providing another way to obtain the same information, the only difference being that the responses are oral, not written.

Some of the federal agencies still using the traditional format applications are also starting to incorporate a structured interview into their SES selection process. They believe they learn important things about the applicant that they would never learn from written statements or a less rigorous "informal" interview. The bottom line, then, is that the SES job applicant today needs to be prepared to describe his or her ECQs effectively in an interview setting, regardless of the application method used for the particular job.

QRB Interview Evaluation Template

The template on the opposite page is used to capture an agency's findings about a candidate's executive core qualifications for the purpose of requesting QRB certification of that individual for initial career appointment to the Senior Executive Service. This template can only be used if a "Structured Interview" was conducted as part of the selection process.

The candidate's relative strength in each of the Executive Core Qualifications is indicated by the ERB or Appointing Authority in the "Rating" column.

Each rating will be made using the 1 through 4 scale indicated below.

1 – Demonstrated executive experience is unusually strong for initial career SES appointee in this area.

2 – Demonstrated executive experience is sufficient to predict success in the SES without early supplemental development.

3 – Demonstrated executive experience is sufficient to predict success in the SES but early supplemental development is planned. (If any ECQ is rated 3, the agency should specify on an attachment the kind of supplemental development planned for the candidate and the schedule on which it will occur.)

4 – Limited demonstrated experience. Targeted developmental plan proposed.

The "Best Evidence" column is used to identify/describe the basis for ratings. Both the demonstrated executive experience and results achieved are to be included in the "Best Evidence" column. The source of that information will be identifed by these initials:

- R (Resume)
- AR (Accomplishment Record)
- I (Interview(s))
- V (Verification)
- O (Other source of information; please specify what this other source of information is, e.g., 360-degree assessment)

The fundamental competencies (interpersonal skills, oral communication, integrity/honesty, written communication, continual learning, and public service motivation) are shown under each ECQ because they are the foundation for success in each ECQ. They need not be addressed directly as long as the presentation, in its totality, shows mastery of these competencies on the whole.

If any ECQ is rated 4, the Executive Resources Board must: 1) identify any special or unique qualities that have caused the ERB to conclude the individual has a strong likelihood of executive success despite the lack of evidence supporting possession of the ECQ; and 2) provide a development plan that stipulates the development strategies the ERB and/or appointing authority will provide within the first year after appointment to strengthen the individual's ECQ to ensure executive success. This strategy must be signed by the ERB chairman and/or appointing authority. A QRB will consider any special or unique qualities identified and the agency's strategy and plan in determining whether to certify the candidate.

Executive Core Qualifications	Rating (1, 2, 3 or 4)	Best Evidence (R, AR, I, V, O—if using "O", please specify the source)
Leading Change		
- Creativity and Innovation - External Awareness - Flexibility - Resilience - Strategic Thinking - Vision - Fundamental Competencies		
Leading People		
- Conflict Management - Leveraging Diversity - Developing Others - Team Building - Fundamental Competencies		
Results Driven		
- Accountability - Customer Service - Decisiveness - Entrepreneurship - Problem Solving - Technical Credibility - Fundamental Competencies		
Business Acumen		
- Financial Management - Human Capital Management - Technology Management - Fundamental Competencies		
Building Coalitions		
- Partnering - Political Savvy - Influencing/Negotiating - Fundamental Competencies		

Behavior-Based Questions

A structured interview often includes behavior-based questions. SES applicants must understand that the major underlying factor in the use of the structured interview is found in the axiom, "Recent past performance is the best predictor of future performance." Behavior-based questions ask about a candidate's past performance, which is an indicator of similar future performance. Behavioral questions ask, "What have you done?" as opposed to, "What would you do?" Evaluators asking behavior-based questions want to hear how a candidate managed a program, not how the candidate would manage a program if presented with the opportunity.

The interviewers are looking for CCAR-type responses—stories of how a candidate led a program and directly effected organizational change with tangible results. Most structured interviews include a set number of questions while within a set timeframe; consequently, candidates need to respond succinctly to questions providing enough context to help the interviewer understand the scope and breadth of the situation; describe the challenges to help the interviewer understand the complexity; describe actions taken to resolve the issue; and describe results—individual results and organizational results.

Behavior-based response to the question, "Describe your ability to manage large funds":

> "As the CIO for my Agency, I accounted for, justified, and administered a $200 million budget before Congress. Specifically, I developed a proposal to justify additional funding of $50 million to ensure IT requirements for warfighters in combat. These systems included smart phones, delivering up-to-the-minute data searches for Soldiers in warzones who, for example, might encounter a new type of IED. Due to budget cuts and freezes, I developed a communications plan and my senior staff met personally with all members of the appropriations committee. It took more than one year, but I successfully obtained the plus up funds, and a plan is in motion now to design and deliver high-level technology to warfighters."

The above response follows the CCAR format and clearly describes the candidate's mastery of his ability to manage large funds and obtain funding to support his programs.

A non-behavior-based response would begin like this: "If I were a manager of funds, I would develop proposals to justify why I would need additional funding to support major programs..."

During the interview process, and even in the application packages, avoid the use of opinions, philosophies, and "How you would do it if you were hired" responses. Phrases to avoid include, "I believe", "I feel", "I think"—these are opinion statements.

What to Expect During a Structured Interview

- The selecting official or designate will do a "read in" that establishes the parameters and expectations of the interview (i.e., time allowed, number of questions, taking notes, holding your questions to the end, and other items).

- Often, the interviewers will ask the candidate, "Tell us a little about yourself," followed by: "What makes you a good applicant for this position?"

- They will then take turns asking questions that have you "describe" your experience in the CCAR format.

- If you leave out any of the CCAR components, they may follow up with a probing question, seeking more information and a more detailed description of that specific component.

- The panel, when done, may ask if you have any questions about the position or agency.

- The interview will close, and the interviewers will thank you for your participation.

A Step-by-Step Approach to Preparing for an SES Behavior-Based Interview

The critical interview preparation steps listed below are based on a curriculum taught at federal agencies throughout the United States to prepare employees for better interview performance. Applicants who completed these steps frequently reported that they were well-prepared, confident, and felt like they "knew the job" as a result.

Step 1: Analyze the Job Announcement Line by Line
Locate the announcement for the position for which you'll be interviewing, or any other job description you've been provided, and analyze each sentence in the Duties section and the TQs of the SES announcement. Be sure to save any announcement for which you apply!

Step 2: Prepare Your Content
Your responses to behavior-based questions are essentially the same as the CCAR stories you developed for your ECQs and accomplishment bullets. Review these stories to prepare yourself for a behavior-based interview. Make sure that you have written at least five stories to prepare for your interview, using examples that are related to the criteria you have analyzed in the job announcement. Then turn each of your ECQ stories into seven or eight talking points that make it easier to practice and memorize your stories. It is important to practice speaking your interview stories so that you will be fluent in and easily remember your best examples.

In the interview, talk about these examples with animation and enthusiasm to demonstrate your past performance in a positive way. Point out how your leadership strategies and skills helped you to succeed.

Step 3: Study OPM's Practical Guide to Structured Interviews

OPM's guide to structured interviews can be found at https://www.opm.gov/policy-data-oversight/assessment-and-selection/structured-interviews/guide.pdf.

Many SES interviews are structured interviews, meaning that the interviewers are trained, the questions are determined in advance (based on the leadership competencies), and each candidate is asked the same questions. A structured interview is used so that it can be objective, enabling the interviewer to score each answer and compare the performance or response of one candidate to that of another.

Step 4: Research the Agency and Office to Learn the Latest Leadership News and Challenges

Research the agency and office carefully. Print pages from their websites. Find and memorize their mission. Discover who their customers are. Try to research any new challenges or changes occurring in the office or agency.

Step 5: Plan and Practice

Don't cut corners! Take the time to prepare properly by following these guidelines:

- Remember that nothing will make you look worse than not knowing what you put on your own resume. Study your resume carefully and be able to speak about it knowledgably.

- Prepare an executive level one-minute response to the "Tell me about yourself" question.

- Prepare three reasons why they should hire you. Memorize these.

- Write at least five success stories to answer behavioral interview questions.

- Prepare three questions for you to ask the interviewer.

- Practice with a recording device, such as a smart phone or video camera. Listen to your voice. Watch your body language. If recording is not an option, consider practicing in front of a mirror or with a friend or colleague who can offer constructive feedback.

Step 6: Be Confident That You Are a Leader

Here are tips to consider before the interview:

- As you prepare to leave for the interview, make sure to take a printed copy of your reference list, paper and pen for note taking, and directions to the interview site.

- Arrive 10 to 15 minutes early for your interview.

- Stand and greet your interviewer(s) with a firm handshake.

- During the interview, be conscious of your body language and eye contact. Crossed arms make you appear defensive, fidgeting may be construed as nervousness, and lack of eye contact may be interpreted as being untrustworthy. Instead, nod while listening to show that you are attentive and alert. Most importantly, do not slouch.

- If you are in a panel interview, keep your eyes moving from person to person slowly. Show that you are engaged with each person.

- Think before you answer and have a clear understanding of the question—if you don't, ask for clarification.

- Express yourself clearly and convey confidence but not over-confidence.

- Adjust your response length based on the number of questions you will be asked. If you are in an hour-long interview and you will respond to five questions, then adjust your responses to about five to eight minutes per response—that provides time for the panel to ask follow-up/probing questions, and time for you to ask questions of the panel at the conclusion of the interview. If the panel will be asking seven questions, then adjust your responses to three to five minutes each. Gauge your time as you move through the interview. If the panelists look bored, yawn, or fidget, cut your example short and move to the results.

- Show a sincere interest in the organization and position.

- Focus on what you can contribute to the organization rather than what the employer can do for you.

- Do not place blame on or be negative about past employers.

- End the interview on a confident note, indicating that you feel you are a good fit for the position at hand and can make a contribution. Emphasize your interest in the position and what you can bring to the organization.

- Thank the interviewer(s) and ask for a business card so that you will have the necessary contact information for follow-up.

- After the interview, promptly and carefully write gracious letters to thank the interviewers for their time and to remind them of the valuable qualifications you bring to the job. Don't miss this last chance to market yourself and highlight your skills relevant to the position!

Preparing Your CCAR Examples

Use the worksheets on the following pages to prepare interview responses for each of the ECQs. You may have already done this for your written ECQs or accomplishment bullets, but going through the process again will help you remember the details for the interview.

Interview Preparation Sheet: Leading Change

Creativity and Innovation | External Awareness | Flexibility | Resilience | Strategic Thinking | Vision

Interview Story Title:

Challenge:

Context:

Action:

Result:

Interview Preparation Sheet: Leading People

Conflict Management | Leveraging Diversity | Developing Others | Team Building

Interview Story Title:

Challenge:

Context:

Action:

Result:

Chapter Ten

SES Candidate Development (CDP) Program Announcement

Read an excerpt in this chapter from a recent Department of Homeland Security (DHS) SES Candidate Development Program (CDP) announcement with an Accomplishment Record Review as part of the application. Top tips for writing the CDP application follows on page 145.

After completing a CDP program where your ECQs are certified by the QRB, don't forget to enroll in OPM's SES Candidate Development Program Opportunities (CDP-Opps) listserv, where you will receive alerts to Government-wide SES vacancies, including on opportunities that appropriately are not announced on USAJOBS.

Enroll at: http://listserv.opm.gov/wa.exe?A0=CDPOpps.

The President has challenged cabinet Secretaries and senior federal agency heads to create a government that is more citizen results oriented and market based. To achieve this vision within DHS, we are searching for high-caliber leaders who possess high standards of excellence and enjoy challenging opportunities to make a difference that impacts our nation.

DHS invites qualified individuals to apply to its prestigious Senior Executive Service (SES) Candidate Development Program (CDP), expected to begin in May 2016. Qualified individuals are those who have demonstrated through their performance and experience the potential to assume executive positions within the federal government.

The SES CDP is designed to develop the talents and skills of individuals with executive potential in order to create a cadre of candidates who can assume senior management positions at the SES level as vacancies occur. Candidates who successfully complete the program and receive certification of their executive qualifications by an Office of Personnel Management (OPM) Qualifications Review Board (QRB) under the criterion of 5 U.S.C. 3393(c)(2)(B), will be eligible for noncompetitive appointment to the SES. Participation in the program does not guarantee placement in an SES position.

Job Title: DHS Senior Executive Service Candidate Development Program
Department: Department Of Homeland Security
SALARY RANGE: $98,633.00 to $158,700.00 / Per Year
SERIES & GRADE: GS-0301-00
OPEN PERIOD: Friday, October 23, 2015 to Thursday, November 5, 2015

HOW TO APPLY:

The application process used to recruit for this program is the **ACCOMPLISHMENT RECORD method**.

QUALIFICATIONS REQUIRED:

To be considered minimally eligible, applicants must meet the requirements described below by the closing date of the program announcement:

The DHS SES Candidate Development Program requires that individuals have at lea dst one year of supervisory experience and have demonstrated exceptional executive leadership potential. Supervisory experience is normally obtained by serving in positions at the Grade 15 level or equivalent.

Your resume must explicitly demonstrate one full year of supervisory experience, including duties and dates. Supervisory experience includes planning, assigning, and evaluating the work of subordinate employees.

All applicants must submit online written statements (narrative) describing your accomplishments against each of the competencies identified below. You must address each competency separately and are required to respond to all competencies. If you fail to do so, you will be rated as "ineligible."

1. **Financial Management** - Understands the organization's financial processes. Prepares, justifies, and administers the program budget. Oversees procurement and contracting to achieve desired results. Monitors expenditures and uses cost-benefit thinking to set priorities. (Business Acumen)

2. **Flexibility** - Is open to change and new information; rapidly adapts to new information, changing conditions, or unexpected obstacles. (Leading Change)

3. **Strategic Thinking** - Formulates objectives and priorities, and implements plans consistent with long-term interests of the organization in a global environment. Capitalizes on opportunities and manages risks. (Leading Change)

4. **Entrepreneurship** - Positions the organization for future success by identifying new opportunities; builds the organization by developing or improving products or services. Takes calculated risks to accomplish organizational objectives. (Results Driven)

5. **Developing Others** - Develops the ability of others to perform and contribute to the organization by providing ongoing feedback and by providing opportunities to learn through formal and informal methods. (Leading People)

6. **Political Savvy** - Identifies the internal and external politics that impact the work of the organization. Perceives organizational and political reality and acts accordingly. (Building Coalitions)

HOW YOU WILL BE EVALUATED:

Click the following link to view the assessment questionnaire, <u>View Occupational Questionnaire</u>.

Candidate Selection Process: The candidate selection process will have several phases.

Phase I: Initial Review of Application Package
An initial review of applications for completeness, basic qualifications, and eligibility. Applicants who submit an incomplete application or are found not qualified will be notified. Applications of qualified individuals will move on to Phase II.

Phase II: Accomplishment Record Review
A panel will rate applications against the six competencies identified above. To ensure fairness and consistency, all applications will be evaluated against the same set of criteria. At this phase, minimally qualified applicants will be further evaluated on the quality and extent of their accomplishments in the six identified competencies. These competencies facilitate potential to master the five ECQs. Applicants will be placed into one of three categories – top, middle, bottom - within their occupational track (e.g. Core, Law Enforcement, etc.). All applicants in the top category will move on to Phase III.

Phase III: Structured Telephone Interview
A panel will rate applicants against five specific competencies. Highly qualified applicants will participate in a Structured Telephone Interview (STI), which will assess candidates' competencies using targeted questions and benchmarks to evaluate responses. Applicants who make it to Phase III will receive an e-mail 2-3 days prior to their scheduled interview. The e-mail will inform applicants on the rules of structured interview and identify the five competencies that will be the focus of the interview. At the conclusion of this process, applications will be ranked and assigned an overall score. Highly qualified applicants will be placed on a selection certificate for selection consideration by all DHS components.

Phase IV: Selection
The ERB will make final selection recommendations based on all available information about the candidate's qualifications, DHS's succession planning needs, and projected future vacancies in the SES.

APPLICATION EVALUATION:

Your resume will be evaluated specifically for:
- Current civilian workforce experience; and
- A minimum of one year of supervisory experience.

You will be evaluated on the quality and extent of your total accomplishments determined by reviewing the Accomplishment Record. Your Accomplishment Record will be evaluated by a rating and ranking panel. Based on application materials provided, best qualified applicants will receive an interview.

Top Tips for Writing Accomplishment Record Narratives from ECQ Writing Coaches

Follow the character length requirement carefully when drafting your accomplishment story. If the length is 3,500 characters with spaces, do not write 7,000 characters. The SES reviewers will not read the lengthy document.

Use the personal pronoun "I" several times in each paragraph, so that the HR reviewers will remember that this accomplishment is something that you led, managed, and completed.

Start out the accomplishment example with your own role in the project. Do not start your narrative with 10 lines of history, background, and/or philosophy. Make an impactful, clear statement about your own role in the project at the beginning of your narrative.

Use the words of the competency, such as political savvy, entrepreneurship, change, people, or results. The HR reviewers will be looking for words that reflect the required competency, and your examples must demonstrate the competencies.

Leave out most of your discussions of meetings and scheduling of meetings. Focus on the challenge of the accomplishment, your actions, and the results. Edit out most (and perhaps even all) of the references to meetings.

Reduce your use of acronyms as much as possible. The acronyms will interfere with the content of the sentence.

Insert numbers wherever possible. If your accomplishment is about finances, insert dollars, amount saved, or the effects of the savings. If the accomplishment is about flexibility, insert the before numbers and the after numbers based on your solutions and recommendations. The dollars and numbers will create a more visual picture of your story and demonstrate the solid metrics of your actions and results.

Add the fact that you met or increased the value of your mission. Make it clear that you are working toward a specific mission in your accomplishments. If you saved lives or improved services for the American traveling public, make it clear and write it. Be specific.

Do not use the words Context, Challenge, Action, or Results at the end of each paragraph. The ERB and QRB reviewers prefer to recognize the narratives based on the content. You can use the words Challenge and Results in the text of the narrative.

Glossary

CCAR: CCAR is the Challenge, Context, Action, and Result storytelling model for describing accomplishments. This model is recommended by OPM for writing the ECQ narratives and is highly effective for framing brief accomplishment descriptions for the five-page resume-based application. The CCAR method can also be used very effectively in preparation for the structured, behavior-based interview.

Cover Letter: A cover letter or letter of interest may accompany a senior executive application package. The cover letter should describe the applicant's interest in the position, provide brief examples of how the candidate's experience is a good fit for the position, and highlight strong leadership qualifications essential to the open position. It should also include the announcement number, position title, and a list of attachments. The cover letter can be one to one-and-a-half pages and could help the candidate to stand out. Check the vacancy announcement to make sure the cover letter does not count against the five-page resume limit.

Executive Core Qualifications (ECQs): The five leadership ECQs determined by the Office of Personnel Management are: Leading Change, Leading People, Results Driven, Business Acumen, and Building Coalitions. Candidates must demonstrate clearly the scope, quality, and level of responsibility sufficient to successfully perform the duties and responsibilities of a senior executive position.

Executive Federal Resume: The executive federal resume is used for applying to GS-15 and SES applications and is prepared in the federal resume format. This resume is, on average, three to five pages and must include relevant Work Experience (from the last 10 years), Education, Certification, Awards, Relevant Training, and accomplishments that demonstrate your leadership skills. The ECQs and TQs do not need to be covered in the traditional format executive federal resume.

Five-Page SES Federal Resume: This is a streamlined, yet comprehensive, federal resume format for SES applications required to be in the resume-based format. This resume can be no more than five pages in length, must include the ECQs within the context of the resume, and should provide information about accomplishments and TQs. This resume also must include your relevant Work Experience (from the last 10 years), Education, Certification, Awards, and Relevant Training.

MTQs/PTQs/MTCs: These are alternate names for Technical Qualifications (TQs): Mandatory Technical Qualifications, Professional Technical Qualifications, Mandatory Technical Competencies, or similar.

Senior Executive Service Candidate Development Program (SES CDP):

This intensive OPM-sponsored program is designed to train, develop, and certify individuals who exhibit outstanding executive potential for SES positions.

Technical Qualifications (TQs): TQs are the Technical Qualifications that agencies require of candidates, specific to the position and agency. TQs may be required in essay format or integrated into the five-page SES resume-based application. Candidates must demonstrate experience and skills sufficient to successfully perform the duties and responsibilities of a particular executive level position.

Index

About the Author
KATHRYN TROUTMAN

Kathryn Kraemer Troutman is the founder and president of The Resume Place, Inc., a service business located in Baltimore, MD, specializing in writing and designing professional federal and private-sector resumes, as well as coaching and education in the federal hiring process. For over 40 years, Troutman has managed her professional writing and consulting practice, publishing and federal career training business, and with her team of 20 Certified Federal Resume Writers, The Resume Place advises and writes more than 300 federal resumes per month for military, private industry, and federal clients worldwide.

Internationally recognized as the "Federal Resume Guru" by federal jobseekers and federal human resources specialists, Troutman created the format and name for the new "federal resume" that became an accepted standard after the SF 171 form was eliminated in 1995. She is the pioneering designer of the federal resume based on her first book, the Federal Resume Guidebook, now in its sixth edition.

Troutman is an in-demand, government contract federal career trainer, who has trained thousands of federal employees in writing competitive federal fesumes, KSAs in the fesume, Senior Executive Service applications, and USAJOBS applications for more than 175 federal agencies in the United States and Europe. Her Federal Career Training courses and publications are listed on the GSA Schedule for government agency purchase. Her popular website, www.resume-place.com, receives more than 50,000 visitors per month, and provides online tools to assist with federal resume writing and federal job searches to jobseekers worldwide.

Troutman created the Certified Federal Job Search Trainer program—the first ever federal career train-the-trainer program for career counselors and military career counselors—using the popular curriculum, Ten Steps to a Federal Job, based on the award-winning book by the same name. Since 2002, more than 500 career counselors and workshop leaders have been licensed to teach the Ten Steps curriculum. In addition, the 62 U.S. Navy Fleet and Family Support Centers worldwide teach this curriculum to separating and retiring military personnel and family members as part of Transition GPS (Goals, Plans, Success). U.S. Air Force, Coast Guard, and Army military transition centers use the Ten Steps Jobseeker Guide (workshop handout) and curriculum to help military personnel write federal resumes and USAJOBS submissions.

Some of Troutman's other federal career publications include the Federal Resume Guidebook, the award-winning Student's Federal Career Guide, and the Military to Federal Career Guide, which is used in every Navy and Marine Corps base and most Air Force career transition centers in the world.

Troutman is a Federal Career Coach to federal, military, and private sector jobseekers who are striving to achieve their first job in government or get promoted. She is a Certified Career Management Coach with specialized expertise in government careers and advises executives in achievement of Senior Executive Service ranks, as well as career management and growth for all career levels.

A frequent radio, TV, and online guest, Troutman answers questions about federal careers, resume writing, and job search techniques.

Diane Hudson

Certified Federal Job Search Trainer & Counselor
SES Strategist, Writer & Trainer
Certified Professional Resume Writer & Coach
Certified Leadership & Talent Management Coach
Federal Government Resumes & Application Procedures Specialist
Military Transition Authority

Diane Hudson is a multi-credentialed career coach and executive resume writer and editor, specializing in posturing federal and non-federal employees to enter the federal government's Senior Executive Service (SES). She is an expert in writing SES and ECQ packages, and coaching and training clients to define their strengths, and persuasively demonstrate writing their decision-making and leadership abilities, by "telling their leadership stories" according to the ECQ leadership competencies/requirements. She skillfully analyzes clients' core leadership qualifications and maps them to the ECQ competencies for submission to the QRB. Diane is a popular and experienced trainer in Federal Resume, SES, ECQ/TQ, and KSA writing topics for SES Leadership Development program candidates at the Naval Ship Yard at Capitol Hill, Air Force leadership, the Defense Acquisition University, EPA, PTO, FEMA, CDC, NRC, U.S. Army Special Operations, U.S. Southern Command, and many other agencies. She also trains military employment readiness specialists and retiring military, and she is a train-the-trainer at industry conferences internationally on outplacement and career search topics.

As an award-winning resume writer, her achievements include "Best Executive Resume" award by the Professional Association of Resume Writers & Career Coaches. Her resumes, cover letters, and case studies are published in more than 60 books and periodicals; she is chapter author on military to civilian transition in the Federal Resume Guidebook, Third, Fourth, and Fifth Editions; chapter author on the SES in the Federal Resume Guidebook, Fifth Edition; and case study author for Ten Steps to a Federal Job, Second Edition. She writes columns and articles for numerous organizations and served as the Veteran Expert for Job-Hunt.Org and as the Federal Expert for Workforce50.com.

Diane formerly held a federal job as a Special Agent Investigator for the Department of Defense, and as a Recruiter/Employment Specialist for Northrop Corporation in Los Angeles, California. She holds a degree in Journalism from California State Polytechnic University, California, and nine career industry credentials. Diane is an active member of the Board of Directors, Professional Association of Resume Writers/ Career Coaches (PARW/CC) and creator and Director of the Certified Professional Career Coach program; and was an active member of the Career Management Alliance, as the monthly Federal Facts facilitator, and winner of the first annual Career Industry Mentor Award. She also serves as an outplacement coach for such organizations as CareerBuilder (Keller School of Management).

Diane has navigated four international moves, living abroad for 12 years and in the Washington, DC/Baltimore corridor for five years.

Paul Thompson

Paul Thompson is a management consultant based in the Washington, DC area. Mr. Thompson retired from federal service late in 2010 after a long and varied career at the U.S. Office of Personnel Management (OPM). Among has many positions at OPM, Mr. Thompson served on the evaluation team for the groundbreaking Navy ("China Lake") pay banding/pay-for-performance demonstration project and later managed demonstration project development, serving as OPM lead for both the NIST performance pay and USDA staffing demonstration projects. The USDA project pioneered the category ranking staffing system that has since become universal across the federal government. Mr. Thompson was also instrumental in developing the first framework for human resource management accountability, and later managed OPM's human capital outreach to several human and natural resource agencies. More recently, he managed Senior Executive Service (SES) policy for OPM, and led a project to establish a resume-based application process for potential SES members.

Mr. Thompson has written several reports and articles over his career, and was the primary author of the first Federal Human Capital Survey summary report in 2002. Since becoming a consultant he has worked with GSA and SIGTARP on SES performance management, and is a Strategic Advisor with the Partnership for Public Service. He is currently designing and implementing a performance management system for the National Labor Relations Board.

A native of Minnesota, Mr. Thompson is married and has two adult sons. He holds a B.A. from Carleton College, an M.A. from the University of Wisconsin - Madison, and an M.B.A. from the University of Maryland - College Park. He is an ardent amateur musician and also enjoys travel, baseball, theatre, and movies.

Get More Expert Help With Your SES Application!

The Resume Place Senior Executive Services Writers and Consultants are experts at preparing various formats that could be required by federal agencies. The total SES package is made up of the following application elements:

- Five-Page SES Federal Resume
- Executive Federal Resume
- Technical & Managerial Qualifications (one page each maximum or TQs might be included in your federal resume)
- Executive Core Qualifications (ECQs) – Leading Change, Leading People, Results Driven, Business Acumen, and Building Coalitions
- Long-Form – Traditional ECQs: 8,000 characters, 10 pages maximum, past 10-15 years of experience, examples for each ECQ, CCAR format
- Short-Form – Leadership Competency ECQs: 5,000 characters, 5 pages max, past 15 years of experience, one long example or two short examples each in the CCAR format
- Executive Cover Letter

More Information:
www.resume-place.com/ses
(888) 480-8265

From the Foreword to the Federal Resume Guidebook, 5th Edition:

"So – what's the savvy job applicant to do? Clearly, they will need to do their homework and pay close attention to the relevant details about the job and the application process contained in the announcement for each federal job in which they are interested. Simply submitting the same boiler-plate resume and cover letter to every job one sees is not going to be nearly as successful as a carefully tailored response that speaks to the specifics of each job.

… **Kathryn Troutman** has literally made a career out of understanding and tracking the evolution of the federal hiring system and translating that understanding into practical advice for the job seeker."

John Palguta
Vice President of Policy
Partnership for Public Service

Free federal career info! >> *Visit www.resume-place.com/resources*

- Free webinars about federal resume and federal career consulting services
- Free webinars on Hiring Reform and how it will affect your federal job search
- Free KSA, Federal Resume, and Cover Letter Builders
- Up-to-the minute federal job search info—register for our informative newsletter
- Federal job search news articles, updated daily

Brought to you by:

Kathryn Troutman
Author, *Federal Resume Guidebook*
President and Founder of The Resume Place, Inc.
The Leading Federal Career Consulting and
Federal Resume Writing Firm in America

Agency-Sponsored
SES ECQ Writing Workshops

This new edition is the official text for our SES ECQ Writing Workshops.

Invite our SES ECQ coaches and instructors to your agency Leadership Development Program or in preparation for important SES applications. Course formats include: one day, two day, one instructor, two instructors, webinar, and follow-on one-on-one ECQ reviews, evaluations, and editing. Provides valuable instruction and inspiration for senior federal managers and team leaders on writing and developing quality written examples for the five mandatory ECQs.

This power-packed workshop covers:

- Writing the Senior Executive Service (SES) Executive Core Qualifications (ECQs)
- Five-Page SES/ECQ Federal Application
- SES Interview Preparation

This same two-day SES ECQ Writing Workshop has been held for: AF, Navy, Army, USMC, EPA, NASA, DOI, USSS, FEMA, DHS, and TSA leadership programs.

Bring this course to your government agency office.

We are a GSA vendor / CCR registered / Small, Woman-Owned Business.

GSA Schedule #GS-02F-0023S

FEDERAL CAREER
Training Institute

More information:
www.fedjobtraining.com
Email us at training@fedjobtraining.com
Or submit a training program request at:
www.fedjobtraining.com/trainingrequest.htm

Award-Winning, Best-Selling Career Books by Kathryn Troutman

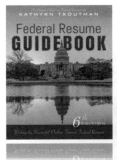 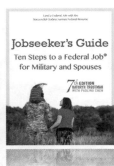   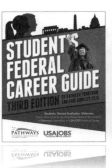 

FEDERAL RESUME GUIDEBOOK 6th Edition—Perfect for federal-to-federal jobseekers. This book has comprehensive, in-depth guidance on how to craft the perfect federal application to change jobs or get promoted. The *Federal Resume Guidebook* is THE book that created today's federal resume.

JOBSEEKER'S GUIDE 7th Edition—The *Jobseeker's Guide* is the first-ever publication for military and family members who are seeking federal employment. This best-selling publication is the accepted training handout in Transition GPS classes and employment courses at Military Transition Centers worldwide and is utilized in more than 100 military bases around the world. This publication is also the featured guide supporting the Certified Federal Job Search Trainer program for career counselors on the Ten Steps to a Federal Job®.

CREATING YOUR FIRST RESUME—If you have never attempted to write a resume, this book has easy instructions and sample first resumes to see how to organize, focus, and format your education and experience into a successful resume.

TEN STEPS TO A FEDERAL JOB 3rd Edition—Wouldn't it be great to have all the basic steps you need to land that dream federal job in just one book? *Ten Steps to a Federal Job* is that book, and with the 3rd edition, Kathryn Troutman outdid herself by adding new crucial details and background on the federal job search that you won't find anywhere else! Learn the tips and tricks to convert your private-industry resume into a winning federal format.

STUDENT'S FEDERAL CAREER GUIDE 3rd Edition—This book is a must-buy for students, new graduates, young professionals, parents, college career centers, and career counselors. Details the winning 10-step process for going from the classroom to a federal job. Includes basics like our federal employment glossary, tips on salary negotiation, and a step-by-step guide to the behavior-based interview.

ALJ WRITING GUIDE—The *ALJ Writing Guide* is mandatory reading for any attorney who would like to apply for Administrative Law Judge positions with the U.S. Government. The examination process for ALJs is among the most complex in all of OPM. Strict adherence to OPM's requirements is essential. These conventions are not spelled out in OPM's announcements but form a central theme of the *ALJ Writing Guide*.

More information, secure online ordering, and bulk orders:
www.fedjobtraining.com/books
(888) 480-8265 ext. 2
Also available on Amazon.com